A Violet Feather

To Alan

I hope you enjoy the read.

Best Regards

Christine
xxx

Kobayaashi

A Violet Feather

by

Hannah C. Stewart

Kobayaashi

A Violet Feather

© Copyright 2024 Hannah C. Stewart

All Rights Reserved. No part of this book may be reproduced or transmitted in any form or by any means, electronic or mechanical, including photocopying, recording, or by any information storage and retrieval system without the prior written permission of the author, or publisher, except where permitted by law.

The events shared through these pages are based on a series of real experiences. Some names have been changed.

First Printed 2024

Published by Kobayaashi Studios www.kobayaashi.co.uk
All enquiries : info@kobayaashi.co.uk

Amazon Edition

The 'upturned K' logo is a TradeMark of Kobayaashi Studios

Cover Design & Artwork by Gillie Whitewolf © 2024

For Cassie

My life was blessed through your friendship.

Saying goodbye wasn't for us.

Every memory and joke shared keeps us forever close.

Hannah

Contents

Encountering the Extraordinary	1
Early Days	8
Sceptics and Signs	17
High Spirits	23
Dave's Story	31
Chance Encounters and Cheese Scones	38
Howard's Story	45
Timely Interventions	54
Tails of the Unexpected	64
A French Connection	69
Shenanigans in the Séance Room	74
Trance Night Revelations	91
A Spirit Calls	98
Everyone has a Story	104
Coming Together	109
Love Was There First	115
A Violet Feather	120
Finding Gold	122
Afterthoughts	126

Encountering the Extraordinary

Startled from sleep by my phone ringing, I irritably shot out of bed and noted the time. 6.30 a.m. The brief irritation faded when I saw my best friend was calling. Then, the pit of my stomach churned; there must be something wrong. She wouldn't usually call me for a chat so early in the morning. Her husband had been unwell for some time; fearing the worst, I took a deep breath and, trying to keep the concern from my voice, cheerily answered,

"Good morning, sweetie. What's up?"

I heard her husband's distinctive Donegal accent, and his voice telling me my beautiful, sassy friend was dead. Shocked and not knowing what to say, I stupidly asked if he was sure, and he told me he was. He had found her fully clothed, lying across her bed, her spectacles still on her face. She seemingly collapsed and died as she was getting ready for bed the night before.

Silence.

Sometimes, our reality changes in a heartbeat. At that moment, my world seemed to fall away, and everything shifted into slow motion. I was aware that my voice was rising, demanding details. I heard the phone being handed over, and then a kind female voice told me she would call later with more information. In the background, I heard someone crying; the phone went dead.

Stunned, I moved into the kitchen and switched on the coffee machine. Waiting for the water to hiss, I walked through the mundane: emptying ashtrays, making the bed, feeding the dog. I pulled back the curtains, and the late May sun flooded the room. The day threatened to be hot.

The pungent aroma of coffee pulled me back to the kitchen. Grabbing a cup and watching the rich, dark liquid hit the frothy milk, the familiar and satisfying daily ritual comforted me. Then, back to the bright sitting room. I sat on the pink overstuffed sofa, sipping coffee and smoking. I stared through the open door into the garden at a single red poppy before finding my voice.

"Wow, how did that happen?"

I expressed disbelief, trying to process the news that my friend was no longer there, but nothing was computing. How could that happen? I was talking to her yesterday, and she was fine. How could she no longer exist? How dare she sneak off without saying goodbye?

Chain-smoking. I understood from working in bereavement support that this strange, shock-like, surreal feeling was temporary and would soon end. Numb and unmoving, two hours passed until I could no longer stomach drinking cold coffee grains, and headed into the kitchen. It was a little after nine.

Knowing I had a client around lunchtime, I made some calls. Checking in with the manager at the charity where I worked was imperative. Hearing her assure me that she would cancel my clients for the foreseeable future, fast-track me into counselling, and that I should expect to be away from my role until I had undergone that journey was a relief. Grateful for the space and time I'd been given, I walked back into the lounge, fresh coffee in hand - and there, standing by the door of my sitting room, was Cassie, my now-dead friend.

Sounds impossible? Yep, agreed. But there she was.

My friend appeared to be standing behind what looked like the transparent film that displays data on overhead projectors. I saw nothing wraith-like or insubstantial about her. Cassie was right there, three-dimensional, smiling widely, and giving me a double thumbs up. Moreover, she looked the best I'd seen her in years. Colour and body had returned to what had become thin white hair in recent years, and her face looked smooth as if every line had been wiped away. She wore her usual clothing, and her missing front tooth was firmly back in place. Then, in a heartbeat, she was gone.

Punching the air, I laughed and shouted, "I saw you!"

My eyes darted over to the empty space she had just filled; I sat hard on the sofa, lit another cigarette, and stared at the void, just in case she came back. I was euphoric. Cassie had done what we had always promised one another - that whoever went first would return and prove there was something after death. Apart from dragging chains and wailing at the bottom of beds in the middle of the night, we agreed that when the time came, anything we could do 'from the other side' to make the other take notice was OK with us both. And she had done it.

What if I was hallucinating?

The thought suddenly slammed into my head like a wrecking ball and stopped any feeling of elation in its tracks. Was I seeing what I wanted to see? I already knew from studies I had read for work that post-bereavement hallucinations are commonplace. It certainly didn't feel like the ones I had had following surgery years earlier, or after the pills I had taken in the dark, dodgy nightclubs of my youth. I'd seen some crazy stuff back then, including rabbits wearing hats, but this was nothing like that.

A quick reality check. Everything seemed reassuringly normal. The dog wasn't talking to me, the walls weren't moving, and no fairies were swinging from light shades. Everything seemed very ordinary, and somewhere inside me, I knew that what I had seen was not something my mind had created to comfort me. It was real.

As the day wore on, the temperature rose uncomfortably high. The oppressive heat was heavy and sticky. By the time it reached its zenith around 3 o'clock, it was blistering, and I threw myself under a cooling shower for the second time that day. The water splashed and chilled me as my emotions fought for supremacy, flip-flopping between devastation and exhilaration. It was the strangest of times.

Friends visited, offering their condolences, and much later, when the sun no longer threatened to incinerate me, my dog Herbie and I went for a long walk. He led me along the river Nene, where poppies had painted the landscape in vivid splodges of reds. Vast and flat, the Cambridgeshire landscape shared our silence as we walked through the long grasses, before we came to rest against an old tree stump. The river was still, its surface broken by a pair of swans gliding regally by, their drab, downy cygnets trailing noisily behind.

Alone, not a soul for miles, here was the privacy to allow the crying. Big, ugly crying, with sobs, gulps, snot and sniffs. The kind of necessary outpouring of emotion that is a cathartic release but not for public consumption. It continued unabated until, from over my left shoulder, I heard,

"I'm right here."

My head bolted round so fast I heard my neck crack. Finding no one there immediately spooked me, and my heart began racing. I jumped up and instantly regretted not bringing my phone, knowing no one knew my whereabouts. There was no response when I cautiously called "Hello". That shifted the fear factor up a few notches. Whoever had spoken was very close. The voice was clear and sounded as if it was immediately behind me.

Alarmed, my eyes shot over to where Herbie was lying, napping in the grass. Reassuringly, he wasn't displaying any behaviour that might suggest someone was lurking in the undergrowth. Perhaps I'd just imagined it. Realising that the sun was sitting low in the sky and it would soon be dark, we began our return, walking quickly, encountering no one en route.

We reached the safety of home as the last light of the day slipped from the sky, confused yet intrigued. I was so sure someone was at the riverbank, perhaps a grumpy fisherman hidden in the reeds and annoyed at our intrusion. My thoughts were chaotic. Accepting that today was not normal, and that my emotions were all over the place, I got into bed, convinced my mind had been playing tricks on me.

The night was hotter than Hades; suffocating and unrelenting. After a few hours of fitful sleep, the same voice from the riverbank came into that liminal place between slumber and consciousness. It was not in my head. It came from a point just behind my left ear, and this time, when Herbie looked up alertly in the direction it had come from, I knew he heard it too.

"I'm right here."

By the time daylight crept around the edge of the curtains, I had been sitting at my computer for a couple of hours, researching everything possible about auditory hallucinations. Fearing some grief-related psychosis ailed me, and without a convenient human to bounce my concerns off, visiting an NHS website was the next best thing, but rather than alleviating concerns, it alarmed me further.

The website informed me that auditory hallucinations (hearing voices or noises that aren't there) may seem real, but they're not. They need attention and could be symptoms of schizophrenic spectrum disorders.

Sitting back in the chair, tired of reading, I stretched and reached for a cigarette.

"Bloody Hell, Cassie! Are you reading this, girl? You've croaked it, and I've gone from a fully functioning, healthy adult to potentially being someone with a severe mental disorder in under 48 hours? Really?"

Glancing back at the computer screen, I noticed another symptom of psychosis was talking aloud to oneself. The site recommended that "it's best to seek professional support right away". Preferring to ignore this, I closed the computer and headed for the coffee machine instead.

Outside the kitchen window, the bird table was busy with parent birds bringing their noisy fledglings for an early morning snack. I watched them as the coffee bubbled reassuringly in the background and let my mind wander. I mused about what I'd seen, the voice I didn't recognise, and why I should be hearing it at all. Later in the local grocery store, having forgotten my glasses, I was squinting hard, struggling to read the ingredients on a packet, when I heard,

"You'll bring your specs next time, won't you?"

It made me jump and mildly irritated, I retorted without thinking,

"I bloody heard you."

Thankfully, there was no one around to bother that I was talking to myself. After paying for the groceries and fleeing the shop, I resolved to find out what was happening.

Early Days

Cassie and I shared a long and healthy interest in the continuation of life after death from the day we first met. Everything we knew we had gleaned from her older sister and a battered old paperback book brought for a few pence from a church jumble sale when we were teenagers. It told of wonders occurring in darkened séance rooms and that the dead weren't dead at all.

Reading this, we decided to hold 'séances' in my bedroom using a whisky glass and bits of paper with 'yes' and 'no' and the letters of the alphabet on them. We hadn't got a clue what we were doing, and the only occurrence of note was when my god-fearing mother walked into the room and found us "cavorting with unnatural things." I was grounded, and Father Damien from the church had to come and bless the house. Luckily, he missed the book as he splashed holy water around my bedroom. It was safely tucked away on a shelf alongside Tom Sawyer, Jane Eyre, and my Famous Five collection.

Father Damien sternly informed Cassie and me that we were committing "the gravest of sins" by trying to "raise the dead" and that we should go to church and confess and ask for forgiveness. Naturally, being kids, we assured him we would, but never did. By the time we reached 15, that battered old book was still being read alongside pop magazines, and one of the first things we did when we left school and started earning money was to see a medium.

We paid the princely sum of 75p each for a reading with 'Wee Nancy' as she was known locally. She was a diminutive Scottish lady whom we visited in the dimly lit room of her council house. We found her courtesy of Cassie's sister, who, after much persuasion, reluctantly agreed to take us as long as we behaved ourselves.

Not knowing what to expect, we climbed the stairs and entered Nancy's back bedroom, which she used for doing sittings. Her heart must have dropped when she saw the pair of us walk in, giggling and nudging each other.

Nancy sat in the shadow of a standard lamp, smoke curled from a cigarette held between her nicotine-stained fingers, and her dark brown eyes stared ahead. She tolerated our juvenile wittering for all of five minutes before raising a hand. We fell silent. Mesmerised by her, I peered through the gloom as she said, looking straight back at me, "I have a man here who says his name is Ernest; he comes with a woman called Emma."

That was enough! I shot off my seat and ran from the room, down the stairs, out the front door, and into the safety of the street. I was only there to see if I would marry Big Jimmy from the butcher's shop. Emma was my great-granny, and the only Ernest I knew was my grandfather. The last time I saw him, when I was four, he was in a coffin.

His funeral was a bleak gothic affair. A bitterly cold January wind cut across skies dark with heavy clouds, made worse by horizontal rain that lashed coffins and mourners alike. As befitted 1950s funeral etiquette, everyone wore all black, no exceptions.

My aged spinster great-aunts, accompanied by my grandmother in her widow's weeds, swooped into the frigid church in unison, like a flock of crows in thick lace mourning veils. The heavy scent of Parma Violet perfume trailed after them. Their collective weeping rose and fell as the thin, watery-eyed priest led the morbid funerary rites so beloved of the church.

Sobs threatened to become wails when Watery Eyes peered down from his lectern through thick incense smoke, and gravely informed the congregation that we should all "be ready because none of us knows when our hour will come." Hiding in the corner of an oak pew, I held tightly to my mother's hand and wondered if Grandad had been ready. He'd looked sick the last time I saw him, as he pressed a shiny half-crown coin into my hand, and now he was in a box. I didn't dare move in case God spotted me and put me in the box, too. With hindsight, I wonder if Watery Eyes was a weirdo who just enjoyed scaring little kids.

That funeral was the catalyst for all my childhood fears surrounding death. Others, no better than the first, only added to it as the aged aunts, of which there seemed to be many, followed my grandfather in rapid succession to the family plot in the cemetery on the hill behind our house. That dog-eared old book *This is Spiritualism* by Maurice Barbanell allayed those fears. It became pivotal to my understanding that something other than the cold, wet, wormy ground awaited us when we died.

Nancy eventually forgave my dramatic exit. Embarrassed by my antics, Cassie's sister was less forgiving and refused to speak to me. Over the years, as we grew into women, Cassie and I visited Nancy often. We really liked her, and she was a wise and accurate medium. She and that battered book were why I was comfortable receiving any sign or communication from my now-dead friend.

The extraordinary encounter felt almost too good to be true, and the nagging doubt that I had imagined it, persisted. Needing reassurance, I texted a friend, Orla.

"I've seen Cassie, and now I'm hearing voices. Suggestions?"

Waiting for a response, my thoughts turned to Bob, a former client. He was struggling to come to terms with the loss of his wife and was two years post-bereavement when I first met him. On medication for depression since her passing, he presented as defeated, and admitted having suicidal thoughts. He seemed deeply troubled during our first session as he shifted in his chair, staring hard at the floor.

"I think I'm losing the plot," he began. "I don't know what is real anymore. I never imagined that losing her would do this to me. I think I'm going mad."

I encouraged him to share with me why he felt that way; he hesitated before continuing.

"You may not believe this, but I can smell her. Not all the time, but every night at the same time, between 10 and 10.30 p.m., I can smell cigarette smoke by the back door. That's where she used to have her last fag of the day before going to bed. That's nuts, isn't it?"

I quickly reassured him it wasn't nuts, and he went on to say that he initially thought it was because her clothes were still around and had smoke on them. He had passed these on to charity, and being a non-smoker, he knew no smoking paraphernalia remained in the house. He had entirely redecorated the room with fresh paint and furnishings. And yet, every night, at the same time, he would smell cigarette smoke and somehow know it was her.

Bob, a straight-talking, plain agricultural worker, was not, he quickly informed me, taken to "flights of fancy" or "anything religious," but was nonetheless conflicted. What was happening was impossible. After all, hadn't he seen his wife dead in her coffin, and the dead can't come back, can they? It flew in the face of everything he had ever believed, and the only answer he could come to was that he was slipping into insanity.

I reassured him again that I certainly didn't think he was mad and that what he was experiencing was often reported after a loved one had passed over. His face showed relief that I was open to hearing about his experiences. He admitted they confused him but didn't frighten him; the familiar smell comforted him. When he asked me my beliefs about 'such things', I answered that I subscribed to an afterlife. Knowing I shouldn't discuss my views with clients, I nevertheless felt compelled to reassure him. Not doing so would deny him the space to ask the questions he needed answers to.

Four further sessions saw him blossom following the disclosure of what he now called his 'visits'. Knowing he wasn't going crazy, he was anxious to explore the possibility of continuing consciousness. He had independently booked a reading with a medium. Careworn when we first met, he seemed younger, relaxed, and more confident with each session. His wife's visits continued, and he looked forward to them, even talking to her and telling her about his day. His G.P. had agreed to begin to reduce his antidepressants. He anticipated that Bob would be free of them within a month. At our last meeting, having just gotten himself a rescue dog, Bob smiled a lot and spoke of hope for the future; he was beginning to heal.

My phone pinging heralded the arrival of a text, pulling my thoughts back to the present.

"Coffee?" It was Orla.

It would be good to see her. She would retain her critical sense, analyse my words, and honestly address possible explanations. Orla had a fantastic open mind and was interested in the afterlife, sitting regularly in the same circle as me. She was also eminently sensible, and I knew I could trust her to be honest if she did think I was losing the plot. Within the hour, she was sitting opposite me, open-mouthed, as I related in detail what had happened.

"Wow, that's amazing!" She said with a massive grin on her face.

"Amazing it may be Orla, but is it real? I heard a disembodied voice, or do I think I heard it because I'm losing touch with reality? To be honest I feel perfectly normal other than this... weirdness, can grief really do this?"

Orla held up her hands and studied me closely.

"Whoa, slow down. So you don't have a problem seeing her. You know what you saw, right? It's the voice that is doing your head in?"

I nodded.

Orla folded her arms and leant towards me.

"OK, first of all, you look and sound normal to me, now which monarch is on the throne?"

Amused, I looked at her and grinned.

"Really? OK Henry VIII?" I winked at her. "Elizabeth, of course."

"Yeah but which one?"

"Geeze, Orla, the second!"

Satisfied, she went on, "OK, good to see you haven't lost touch with reality or your sense of humour. So you don't recognise the voice? It's not Cassie's? Yet you readily accept what you saw? Indeed, that might have been a hallucination, too?"

"I agree. Thats why I'm so conflicted. What I saw wasn't a hallucination. Of that, I'm sure. I'm aware that seeing is not necessarily believing. Visual illusions can distort our perception so what we see does not correspond with what is physically there. Yet I just know it was real Orla, I know it in my gut. The voice I'm less certain of, it doesn't sound familiar, certainly not Cassie. If I am imagining the voice, then maybe I imagined what I saw."

"Is the voice male or female? Does it have an accent?" Orla asked.

"Benign, neutral, with no discernable accent, and I couldn't even say what gender it is. I think the one I heard in the shop might have been Cassie, but only because it's the type of thing she would say. I was always forgetting my specs and asking her to read things for me, but it didn't sound like her."

"Are you hearing the voice inside your head?"

"No, it appears to be external, and comes from somewhere just behind my left ear." I pointed to the place. "It's not even a whisper; it's clear as day, and Herbie heard it the second time it happened."

"Are you hearing a spirit, do you think?"

"Maybe, how would I know what a spirit voice sounds like? I haven't a clue. One minute I'm confident of what I saw and heard, then doubt creeps in."

We drank coffee, smoked, and mulled over my sanity, eventually agreeing that I appeared normal, whatever that meant, but accepting that I seemed to be hearing something otherworldly. The conversation veered off to things other than voices from the ether before returning time and again to the voice.

At around nine o'clock, my phone began ringing, displaying a number I didn't recognise that consisted of a string of eights and zeros. Intrigued, I clicked on the receiver and said "Hello" several times but only got back static. I was about to ring off, when the static stopped, and the voice I had heard before said "Goodbye."

The phone went dead, and looking over at Orla, I exclaimed, "It's just happened again, the same voice said goodbye!"

Excitedly, I showed her the number now stored on my phone. She immediately insisted on returning the call. After several attempts using both our phones and getting only persistent static that eventually clicked off, we gave up. A search using Google yielded zero results for that number.

Orla looked at me wide-eyed. "Wowzer! That is just barmy. How does that happen?"

I shrugged my shoulders. "I don't know, but I'm glad you were here when that happened. It's not in my head, is it?"

"No Hannah it's not in your head."

After Orla left, I realised that potentially thousands of people had experienced the confusion Bob and I had. Indeed, we weren't the only ones. How many others were under the impression that they were somehow unwell and possibly taking medication unnecessarily? I also understood the relief and solace Bob must have felt when he knew he wasn't hallucinating.

Sceptics and Signs

The following day, feeling buoyed, and confident that my sanity was intact, I visited a florist before popping into the office to chat with my boss and friend, Bex. She showed me to a private room and got me a coffee. We discussed how I was and the charity's procedure for bereavement leave. I'd been there for about twenty minutes when I dropped the bombshell about what I had experienced. Bex's face immediately betrayed concern. In spite of us being alone, she nevertheless lowered her voice and almost whispered.

"Hannah, are you OK, have you seen your GP?"

"Of course not. Do you think I should?"

"God, Hannah, that's a hell of a question. My head says yes if it continues, you know, just to check you are OK. As you are aware, hearing things isn't normal. You appear fine to me. But..."

"But what?"

"What if you don't know that you need help? Do you feel OK mentally?"

"I'm not howling at the moon, if that's what you mean. I feel fine. Smoking too much, of course. The loss feels overwhelming, but it does not warrant medical intervention.

Bex, I saw Cassie as clearly as I see you now. I didn't imagine it." I said almost defiantly before continuing. "This has made me realise that surely there is a place within bereavement counselling where we should be discussing such things because if I'm experiencing it, surely so are others?"

Bex ignored my comments about discussing similar phenomena within counselling and continued, "I don't know what to say to you, Hannah. Cassie's death was so sudden; you do accept that she has died, don't you?"

I felt insulted.

"Of course! But I also know what I saw; I saw her spirit."

Bex's eyes shot towards the door, as if looking for a way out or someone to rescue her. Her face was blank as she looked back at me. "You've had a shock..."

Frustration rose up in me.

"STOP! Just stop right there; don't say what I think you are about to say."

I felt stupid and could sense her pity, which I hated.

Looking awkward, Bex checked her watch, giving me the perfect opportunity to leave. I muttered something about not wanting to intrude any more on her time. She looked relieved. Her last words, "We'll get you into counselling ASAP," rang in my ears as I self-consciously left the room, almost embarrassed that I'd mentioned my experience. I saw how irrational my words must have sounded to her.

Being told by a colleague that they have seen their dead loved one must be staggering. How do you respond to that?

Bex wasn't alone in her scepticism. I quickly realised that many people found discussing this topic uncomfortable and often perceived it as a sign that the recipients of similar interactions are emotionally off-balance.

Later that morning, Obi and Effie Scoffer, two dear friends, called on me. The three of us had met years before at college and had been firm friends ever since. We shared many interests, particularly travel. The one subject we could never agree on was anything remotely paranormal. Both were huge sceptics, and we had many good-natured debates about life after death. Obie, in particular, was very vocal about his doubts about the authenticity of mediums who, according to him, were all charlatans.

Their response was entirely expected when I revealed happily that Cassie wasn't dead because I'd seen her in my sitting room. A look of horror passed between them, followed by an embarrassed silence.

Effie disappeared into the kitchen, and Obie, always gentle and caring, cautiously asked if I could have imagined it. After further discussion, I accepted that yes, I could have imagined it, but knew I hadn't. My friends teased that, in spite of seeing things, I was otherwise safe to be around and suggested joining them on the river for the weekend. An invitation I eagerly embraced.

That afternoon, we three, Herbie and their dog Banjo, boarded *Beautiful Day*, a sixty-four-foot canal boat home to Obie and Effie that was moored at the embankment in the cathedral city of Peterborough. Once settled, we headed off through the Cambridgeshire Fens along dykes constructed by Dutch workers in the 1700s. Their endeavours had revealed flat, peaty, nutrient-rich land, giving the UK its breadbasket that's still agriculturally important today.

Sitting on the back of the chugging barge, I watched Red Kites swoop and soar with abandon in the endless azure sky. The water lapping gently against the boat soothed me. A cooling breeze wafted over my skin as our journey meandered sedately along waterways historically used for transporting goods. We cruised past feathery reeds, vast plains of hedgeless fields, and those iconic bygones of another era, the black wooden windmills. Eventually, intending to take the dogs for a walk, we stopped and moored the boat on a towpath beside an old church in a small Fenland town.

The little elevated greenstone church stood serenely in the sunlight, its porch covered by tangled honeysuckle. Bees, attracted by the heady, sweet scent, buzzed and danced in the still air. A charming gothic wrought iron gate enticed us along a noisy gravel pathway shaded by giant elm trees into the adjacent graveyard.

Hanging back to read headstones, I was drawn to a raised white tomb; sun-blanched angels, heads bowed in an attitude of prayer, guarded each corner. Compared to many other graves that were crooked, covered in moss, and which appeared neglected, this one looked out of place, like it hadn't been there long. The inscription on the smooth white surface told me the memorial was erected by a father whose son had died in World War Two. Around the base were beautiful words. It was clear that the gentleman had been grieving for a long time.

A movement to my right made me aware that a small tortoiseshell butterfly had alighted on the plinth I was reading. Taking little notice of it, I continued reading and moved to the second side. The butterfly followed, landing right before me. The same happened on the third side. With my curiosity piqued, I wondered if this was one of those incidents that some folk take to be a sign from their loved ones. Quickly checking that I was alone in the graveyard, I whispered, "If that's you, Cassie, take off now and meet me on the other side."

Cassie strongly believed that the spirit world sent signs to those who needed them in the form of birds, feathers, or butterflies. She favoured robins as being a sign that her mother was around. Aware that many people shared this belief, until that moment, my personal bias was that these occurrences had natural origins. Birds fly and shed feathers, and butterflies are common in summer, but when I got to the tomb's fourth side, the butterfly, just as requested, sat as if waiting for me. Somewhat taken aback, I stared at its reddish-orange and black forewings quivering in the sun for what seemed like ages.

Obie and Effie were nearly out of sight, and Herbie, anxious to follow, was pulling on his lead. Unable to move, unwilling to leave, wanting to stay in that precious moment, through tears I said, "You need to go now sweetie because I'll stay until you do. I can't walk away and leave you here."

With that, the butterfly rose and flew straight into my face, alighting briefly on my left cheek before taking off. Stunned, my eyes followed it as it disappeared.

Deep in thought, I led Herbie through a low-arched wooden gateway into the meadow beyond, anxious to catch up with my friends. Knowing their scepticism, I didn't mention the butterfly acting unnaturally. Instead, I hugged the incident to myself, only sharing it a few days later with Orla, who smiled widely and thought it was a beautiful sign.

The weekend was a joy; my friends had gifted me much-needed space and quiet, unlike the following days, which became a blur of emotional exhaustion in the run-up to Cassie's funeral.

When that day eventually arrived, it was mid-June and made memorable because of the horrendous heat. The UK Met Office had warned it would be a hot day, and they weren't wrong. The mercury climbed fast and showed no signs of stopping. The temperature eventually reached a high of 34°C as I stood uncomfortably outside the crematorium with wet hair and sweat dripping down my back, waiting for the hearse to arrive.

Everyone sweltered. Inside, the air conditioning brought some relief to all. Finding a seat, I picked up an order of service book with Cassie's smiling face on the front that had been placed on the chair. Upon opening it, a small tortoiseshell butterfly fell from the page. It was dead but otherwise perfect; its gossamer wings pressed like a flower between the covers. Picking up the fragile creature and gently placing it into a tissue, I put it into my bag. More than a dead insect, it was unique and meant something to me; only then did I see how wrong I had been to reject such signs out of hand.

High Spirits

The immediate aftermath of Cassie's passing was brutal. I missed her physical presence, but regularly felt it, especially when driving. Depending on my mood, sometimes I would berate her for having left without warning, like she had a choice in the matter. Mainly, I just chatted about my day.

Even after so many years as friends, we still had things we wanted to say to one another. The laughs, lengthy phone calls, lunch dates, and intimate girly gossip were absent now, and I tried not to feel sad. After all, nearly half a century of friendship was worth celebrating. The void she left was filled with memories that made me laugh, like the first time we had got drunk together in the Fiddlers Elbow, a grotty old spit and sawdust pub, its walls yellowed by tar from cigarette smoke that hung in the bar like a cloud.

We were fifteen, working in a shoe factory with money to spend, and had lied to the pub landlord when he questioned our age. We had yet to taste alcohol apart from the odd Cherry B or Babycham at Christmas family gatherings. Cassie confidently pointed out a bottle and reliably informed me she had seen it advertised on television. It tasted like aniseed balls, so we should try it, she insisted.

Mixed with blackcurrant, the Pernod tasted fine. The pungent liquorice taste was sweet and warm, belying its potency. Perched on high stools at the bar, feeling immensely grown up, we drank a lot of it and quickly got drunk. Its effect on our young stomachs was devastating. To the amusement of the other patrons, mainly sulphur-smelling men in donkey jackets from the local steelworks, synchronised vomiting ensued as we staggered through the pub to get to the toilets.

Hot on our heels, dancing around the purple spatters of vomit we had generously deposited on the floor, was the landlady, a big blonde Glaswegian woman with arms like Popeye and tattoos to match. We made it to the toilet, emptying the remaining contents of our stomachs into the wash-hand basins before being ejected unceremoniously from the premises with the landlady's parting shot, "Yer barred for life!"

We giggled over that drunken episode as we recalled it down the years. Laughter played a big part in our friendship. So when inexplicable yet playful things began happening after her passing, I was amused and wondered if my friend was still having fun with me.

Objects would disappear, and reappear where they shouldn't be but couldn't be missed, usually in the middle of the floor. Ornaments would be turned around. Getting into bed one night, I found a round tea bag perfectly placed on the pillow. It made me laugh out loud. Had I become so absent-minded as to put a tea bag on my own pillow? Lights I knew I had turned off before bed were on in the morning, spectacles would go missing and be found in plant pots or the middle of the bathroom floor, and the television sprung into life on more than one occasion.

Once, I heard a crackling noise from the sitting room. I

popped in and saw my cats and Herbie asleep on the sofa. Bizarrely floating in mid-air by the window about head height, there were two white, pulsating tic-tac-shaped things; they shot quickly off towards the front door, swiftly followed by a loud bang, and I realised all the electrics had been turned off. These incidents made me smile; I never considered that I was imagining them, and whenever they happened, not knowing why, I diligently recorded them in a notebook.

They all happened within the first six months of Cassie's passing, becoming less frequent as her first anniversary approached. By the time that arrived, they seemed to have stopped altogether. There were no more power outages or teabags in the bed. Keys no longer disappeared and reappeared in the washing machine, as they had once done. It felt right that this should happen, and I hoped she was having the best life ever somewhere.

At that time, I went to see my friend Sally, who had recently moved into her forever home after years of moving around because of her husband's career in the RAF. We did the guided tour, and when I'd seen the new house and admired the garden, coffee in hand, we settled down. We chatted about family, retirement, grandchildren, and, of course, Cassie's sudden death. The post-mortem showed that the culprit was undiagnosed heart disease. I mentioned that things had disappeared and reappeared in my house since her passing. Still, knowing Sally's scepticism, I stopped short of mentioning the flying tic-tac incident. Instead of the expected disbelief from my sceptical friend, she listened and said, "I believe you."

I nearly fell off my chair.

"I believe you because something happened recently, and I can't explain it."

"I'm all ears." I said, lighting a cigarette. This was going to be interesting.

"OK, sounds mad, but here goes."

Sally looked at me and laughed, almost embarrassed. "The only thing I had from my mum after she passed away was a locket with a picture of her and my dad inside. Dad died when I was four, and it was the only picture in existence of him, so it was really special to me. I treasured it and hung the locket and chain over a picture of Mum. When I noticed it was missing one day a couple of years after she died, I was horrified and searched high and low, including the kid's toy box, but it had disappeared. I got used to packing and unpacking our belongings with the frequency we moved. Each time I looked for the locket, I eventually gave up on ever finding it."

Getting up, Sally went to the bifold doors at the back of the house. Turning around, she said, "Now, this is the weird part. A few days after moving in, I had been pottering around the garden and returned to the house through these doors. I was stood right here."

Pointing up, she went on, "As I glanced up at the photo wall, I saw the locket on that frame up there holding my mother's picture! My eyes nearly fell out! Those pictures had only been put up the day before. Surely I would have noticed the locket had it been on there?"

"You would have thought so, absolutely. Wow, that is

amazing."

Sally went on, "It wasn't tangled or caught. It was as if somebody had just draped the chain over the corner of the frame. I grabbed it; it was the same locket containing the precious photograph. It's like it never went away."

She gave me the locket, and I gave it a brief look before returning it to her.

"Interesting," I said. "Maybe you just couldn't see it."

Sally looked at me. "What do you mean?"

"Maybe the spirit world took it away for safekeeping," I said. "Where do you think it's been all these years?"

Sally rolled her eyes at me. "I haven't a clue, where it came from or has been. That isn't important. What matters is that it has come back to me. It was always the picture that was more important. It's so tiny, but one of Brian's mates is a photographer, and says he will do something wonderful with it. I'll always have a copy in case it goes missing again."

"I reckon your mum decided to hold on to it until you got settled." I said.

"You know I don't usually subscribe to such beliefs, but this has made me wonder. Do you believe that stuff disappearing and reappearing at yours was down to Cassie's ghost?"

"She's not a ghost!" I said defensively. "Sure, something has been happening, but I have no proof one way or the other; a couple of times, I have thought I was losing it or, at best, have become really forgetful. A teabag in the bed? What's that about? Your story is fascinating; it reminds me of a very similar one that my friend Prem experienced several years ago:

"His sister-in-law had gifted his wife a tiny Jade Ganesha. Ganesha is the elephant-headed God, widely revered among the Indian community. This small representation of him was kept on the couple's home altar, which they used for morning prayers. It stayed there until one day, about ten years later, Prem's wife noticed it was missing. Naturally upset, she practically turned the house upside down, searching for it. However, the search was in vain. Prem assured her that he would get her another one. But she insisted she didn't want another. That Ganesha was unique from her sister and couldn't be replaced.

"Prem's wife developed cancer and sadly lost the battle with the disease soon afterwards. A few months after her passing, he had made the bed one morning and walked around to the side where his wife once slept. As he smoothed the sheets about halfway down the bed, he saw a tiny Jade Ganesha. Picking it up, he recognised it as the one that had gone missing because of a memorable scratch on its base. The bed had been changed many times, and he now lived alone, so he had no idea how it had gotten there. Overjoyed with his find. He told me he never doubted that it had come from his wife, especially as it was discovered on his birthday. Moreover, he said he had never wondered how such a thing could happen because, like you, Sally, he was just happy it had."

Sally appeared to be thinking.

"It's really weird and has made me wonder. I know that locket wasn't where I found it a couple of days before."

"And then you find it where you can't miss it." I said, "So it's grabbing your attention, which I think is what it's designed to do."

"Talking of grabbing attention, I think you might be right, Hannah. Someone at work was telling me that a similar incident happened to her. When she returned from a holiday in Australia, a second reminder about her routine mammogram was awaiting her. It was due before her trip, and she chose to wait until she got back. On her return, instead of making the appointment, she decided to defer until she was less busy. Sitting on the sofa a few nights later, a picture of her deceased sister fell off the wall and landed face-up beside her. Now, my colleague is a bit like you, Hannah."

Amused, I said, "Whatever do you mean?"

"You know spooky stuff, she believes all that malarky. Because her sister had breast cancer, she took that as a sign from her that she should get checked out. The next day, she made the appointment, and guess what?"

"They found something?"

"Yep, despite having no symptoms, they found cancer, and in the same place her sister had it. She's had treatment and is all good now, but how strange is that? She says it was the picture falling down that made her get checked. It had been hooked onto the wall, and the hook remained in the wall. She is sure it couldn't have 'just fallen'. What do you think?"

"You know what I think, Sally? She's right. Her sister grabbed her attention and it worked. It was urgent, and without that, she might not have gone until too late."

Laughing, I put on a spooky voice, "Spirit works in mysterious ways, don't you know?"

Driving away from Sally's later, I smiled, happy that she had been reunited with her beloved photograph and locket. Prem and Sally were delighted, accepting without question the inexplicable events that had occurred to them. In a way, I envied them; I needed more. Maybe it was more critical now to prove to myself that life went on, and I wondered if that, coupled with a desire to see Cassie, caused me to hallucinate.

I needed to know.

Dave's Story

A chance conversation with a friend, Dave, from Ohio, a few days later revealed that if I had hallucinated, I wasn't alone. When I mentioned having seen Cassie, and my concerns that I had perceived what I wanted to see, Dave said he had experienced an encounter not unlike mine when his brother died following a long illness.

"My brother had passed away the previous afternoon, and the following morning I woke up, went to the kitchen, and began to prepare breakfast. I noticed a soft white glow by the kitchen sink. As I watched it, the light increased in size, acquired depth and began taking my brother's form. Unafraid, I was fascinated by what I was seeing. Within seconds, my brother was standing in front of me. He had been bald since he was 23, and I immediately noticed he now had a full head of hair. He looked very healthy and appeared to have gotten younger by at least 30 years. Everything about him was so vibrant, and I said aloud, "Dude, death looks good on you!" He responded with, "It feels good too." I then said, "Well, have a good afterlife." He smiled and said, "Oh no, death is the beginning of life." At which point, he disappeared."

Blown away by Dave's story, I had questions.

"Wow, how lovely for you," I said. "What were your immediate thoughts? Did you think you were seeing things?"

"Initially, I thought, well, that was an interesting manifestation of grief, to say the least. Most of my family are involved in some area of psychology, grief counselling and therapy, so I knew stuff like that could happen from hearing them discuss such things. But then, within five minutes of that happening, my phone rang. It was a good friend of mine from the area where I live. She had never met my brother, as he lived in Phoenix, 2,000 miles away from me. My friend said, "I had to call you and tell you this. I think your brother just came and visited me. He was with an angel." She went on to describe exactly how my brother looked when I had seen him minutes before!

"That gave me a great sense of peace about my brother's passing. I had gone to Phoenix a few weeks before he died, and we had talked. He told me how scared he was. Here was my big brother, who was never afraid of anything, admitting to being frightened! I believe he came to see me knowing that our last visit had scared me and wanted to reassure me he was now OK. I suspect his guardian angel or guide took him to my friend's house so that she could unwittingly confirm that it wasn't just a manifestation of grief; therefore, I couldn't doubt that my dead brother had been in the kitchen and spoken to me."

"And now? Do you ever look back and question it?" I asked.

"No, I haven't questioned it since. In fact, as time has passed, the real peace that the incident gave me about the afterlife has grown. Afterwards, when I mentioned my brother's passing, and people offered condolences, I'd say, "Oh no, he's fine, don't worry about it." It sounds comical, but that's precisely how I felt and still do. It's as if he just moved to a different address, and of course, I will see him again someday."

Realising that such events were in no way exceptional was both surprising and comforting. I knew Dave was credible, and hearing his story went a long way to easing my fears about my own experiences being a figment of my imagination. It raised the question of how common such incidents are.

To find the answer, I emailed most of my contact list, explaining that I was researching the possibility of after-death communication following bereavement. To ensure I didn't just target people who I knew shared my beliefs, I included colleagues with whom I'd never discussed an afterlife and friends who, to my knowledge, had no interest in such a subject. The questions were as follows:

> Have you ever experienced happenings around the time of a bereavement that you considered might be from your loved one?
>
> What happened that convinced you your loved one was around? (Give as much detail as you are comfortable with.)
>
> How soon after the bereavement did things happen?
>
> Did the experience help with your grief journey?

Conflicted, plucking up the courage to hit send took a while. Concern that people would think I was a weirdo was displaced when, over the following few days, more and more responses to my email dropped into my inbox, revealing that I had underestimated the prevalence of these experiences.

Not everyone replied, but it became apparent that every individual who did had unique stories that they found inexplicable, and that they felt suggested intervention from a non-physical source. They included, amongst others, vivid dreams in which a conversation with the loved one was held, unusual animal or insect behaviour, feathers appearing out of nowhere, auditory (voices or sounds) phenomena, communication through electric devices (e.g., flickering lights, radios coming on), communication through telephones in which the voice of the deceased was heard speaking, lost things being found, seeing and smelling the person, sensing that they were around and being touched, and hearing meaningfully timed songs associated with the deceased.

The one thing all respondents shared was how these incidents had helped them through their grief journey. Like Vinny, whose mum, before her passing, had assured Vinny and her sister that if there was life after death, she would send a white feather.

Vinny wrote that she and her sister had subsequently received white feathers that turned up in unusual places. They helped her "not just with that overwhelming grief of those first few days, weeks, and months, but also so many times over the years when I am sad, need answers, or feel nostalgic. Almost always, I'll find a white feather. I have tried using rationale to explain some of these on one or more occasions. Although I am interested in life after death, it can be hard not to question or to accept it when there can be another explanation, but I always come back to why? Why here? Why now? Why when I am feeling like this?"

Vinny wasn't alone in trying to rationalise the feathers she received. Most respondents stated they had attempted to explain events before concluding that their experiences were down to imagination or coincidences.

I knew from previous studies I'd done, that in the last 50 years there has been an increase in the amount of research undertaken by psychologists on post-bereavement hallucinations of the dead, or, as Freud called them, "hallucinatory wishful psychosis."

One of the earliest was in Wales in 1971 by Dewi Rees[1], who conducted interviews with 227 widows and 66 widowers registered with his general practice in Wales. To his surprise, he discovered that almost half the people he spoke to disclosed that they had experienced hallucinations of their dead spouse, most commonly as a "sense of presence" of the deceased, visual, auditory and tactile experiences.

Most of those reporting encounters regarded them as helpful in their recovery from loss. Rees concluded that these hallucinations (a term I increasingly felt was inappropriate due to its association with mental illness) were normal and beneficial accompaniments of widowhood. He also discovered that 27 percent of interviewees had never shared their experiences with others because of their concerns that they were due to psychological weakness.

"I've never told anyone this before" was common in the responses I received. The fear of not being believed, or of being perceived as deluded or unwell, was real, and one I certainly could identify with. This is understandable when

---

1   W. Dewi Rees, 'The Hallucinations of Widowhood,' *British Medical Journal* (1971)

such incidents are largely incompatible with mainstream conceptions of reality. Nevertheless, they were comforting and meaningful to the recipients.

Confident that my experiences were real, I became less afraid to mention them. Being open encouraged others to speak. I encountered people who, like Steph, a work colleague, said, "Something I can't explain happened."

She shared the following story with me:

"I was good friends with my neighbour across the street. We were young wives with kids around the same age, and we became close. She developed cancer, living only a year after her diagnosis. She was 35. About three weeks after her passing, I looked out of my window and saw the family car pull up on her drive. I watched her husband and three children exit the vehicle and wondered how they were all doing. They walked up to the front door, entered, and closed it behind them. Then, remarkably, I saw my friend leave the car and walk to the door a few seconds later. I couldn't believe it, but knew it was her. I knew because she turned, looked directly at me, and waved. Then she turned and kind of melted through the closed door.

"It brought me so much happiness! I felt as if she was telling me everything was OK. I kept what I'd seen to myself. It gave me a lot of comfort. I never told anyone for years because I didn't want them to steal my joy by telling me what had happened was impossible."

By now, my physical notebook had become a growing digital file of unexplained occurrences; the responses revealed that these inexplicable events were more common than anticipated. Most happened in the immediate three months following a passing, and a few continued long after, on significant dates or, in Vinny's case, when she needed it.

Chance Encounters and Cheese Scones

After working most of our lives, semi-retirement in our fifties had gifted Cassie and me precious free time. Time we regularly used 'for girl treats'. We randomly picked a destination and headed by train or car for 'lunch and a look around'. I missed our lunch trips, so on a whim, I decided one day to go to York for a coffee.

We both loved the city with its narrow medieval streets, overhanging half-timbered shops, and great eateries. Our excursions always included first-class rail travel, and in keeping with that tradition, I bought a ticket online, grabbed a book to read, and headed for the station.

Thankfully, it was relatively quiet. The few passengers on the platform stood locked into their phones. Glancing up at the destination display board, I saw that there were only four minutes to wait. As it snaked into the station, a low rumble heralded the train's approach. The engine hissed to a stop, and as I stepped up into the carriage, a quick look revealed one other passenger, a young man immersed in something on his laptop. Good, I was in a reflective mood, and quiet was the order of the day. The forward-facing seat, upholstered in regal blue and gold, was spacious and comfortable. A selection of daily newspapers and a beverage menu on the table informed me that coffee was complimentary, an added bonus.

An automated recording warned passengers on the platform to avoid the edge and that the train doors were closing. In the distance, a whistle blew as the engine kicked into motion. Moving slowly, the train rumbled along the tracks, quickly gaining momentum as we left the city behind.

I placed the book I had brought with me face up on the table. Tucking myself into the seat, I got comfortable. As we headed North, the landscape changed from flat agricultural fields into curving hills dotted with lush trees. A friendly young steward approached and asked if I wanted a drink. With coffee ordered, my gaze returned to the window. Outside, a vixen lying in the sun, nursing her cubs against a dry stone wall, delighted me.

The coffee tasted all the better for being served in a china cup instead of the usual disposable cardboard. As I drained my drink, a movement to my right stole my attention. A man was standing by the table, indicating the seat opposite and asking me in a broad Yorkshire accent if it was taken.

I wondered why he had picked that specific seat, as plenty of others were available. Having sought a quiet space, I felt slightly annoyed and wanted to say, "No, please don't sit there." Yet, without looking up, I heard myself say the seat was free. Within minutes, the young steward had returned, enquiring if drinks were needed.

The man opposite ordered black tea, and I had another coffee. Not in the mood for small talk with strangers, the book gave me something to hide behind. I pretended to read, not taking in any words.

Finally, I put it down and returned to watching the countryside outside. And then the man opposite spoke.

"That looks like an interesting read."

Oh God, I thought, he's speaking to me, and what's more, I can't ignore him.

Looking across at the stranger, I saw brown eyes surrounded by wrinkles smiling back at me. His thick grey hair matched the colour of his trim goatee beard. He wore a green check shirt, open at the neck, that revealed a dashing mustard cravat partnered with an olive green corduroy jacket peppered with small pin badges on one lapel. I smiled to myself when I saw the same subtle political one I had on a coat at home.

"Yes," I heard myself say, "it's something I'm interested in."

"Me too," he said.

Somewhere around my solar plexus, I felt a tug. It was something I had felt a couple of times in the past when meeting new people who had later become close friends, and I warmed to the man on the other side of the table. I relaxed into my seat and returned to pretending to read. The book was about the life of a Scottish medium.

The train stopped at Loughborough, and my gaze fell on the comings and goings of the people outside on the platform, hurrying away to lives I would never know. As the train began to pull out of the station, the man started talking to me again.

"Are you going to York?" He asked.

"Yes, I am."

"Somewhere special?"

"Betty's Tea Rooms. They make the best cheese scones ever. A cheese scone is not a cheese scone unless there is an heroic amount of cheese in it and Betty's doesn't disappoint on that score."

To which he replied, "I know the place. I hope you've booked; it's always busy."

"Indeed I have."

"They sometimes have a pianist playing upstairs."

"Yep, that's the place, but to be fair, I'm a bit of a philistine when it comes to music; it's the food I go for."

"Are you treating yourself?"

Awkward.

Was this man friendly or nosey? I didn't want to say yes or no. In fact, I didn't want to give this stranger any more details, and yet heard myself saying, "Not so much a treat, having fun with memories. It's a tad eccentric, travelling all this way for coffee and scones, but some things are worth the effort."

We smiled at each other, and I hoped that the man had enough information and would leave me alone. My gaze returned to the window, and a few minutes of silence passed, but he wasn't done talking.

"Have you ever seen him doing a live demonstration?"

I looked up and saw that he was pointing at the book now lying on the table.

Glancing down, the medium's face stared back at me. I heard myself say that I hadn't, but hoped to one day.

The man, oblivious to my desire to be uninterrupted, began telling me he had the great fortune to have seen him and, what is more, had received an evidential reading. The rest of the journey sped by, and despite my early reluctance to talk, I found myself chatting easily with the stranger about life-after-death studies.

At some point in the conversation, the man told me his name was Howard, a former research scientist who worked for a large environmental organisation. He was a widower currently living with a badly behaved parrot called Barney and two rescue dogs.

In turn, my usual disinclination to reveal personal details evaporated. I disclosed that I was collecting stories about spirit interactions with the living and how that interest had started, which seemed to captivate him. All too soon, the train began to slow, and the Victorian grandeur of York Station came into view. Howard opened the battered brown clamshell briefcase that accompanied him and said, "I have a story you might be interested in; perhaps I'll tell you all about it one day, but there needs to be more time than we have now."

Reaching into the case, he brought a card out and handed it to me. "You can contact me via this number if you want to hear it."

Relief swept over me. Thank goodness this lovely man wasn't going to suggest accompanying me to Betty's, which I had anticipated he might and would have had to refuse.

I thanked him, assuring him I'd love to hear his story. As we alighted from the carriage, he turned to me, shook my hand, and said he hoped to hear from me soon. Clutching his briefcase to his chest, he strode purposefully into the crowded station. As I watched him walk away, something inside made me smile, and I hoped it wasn't the last time I would see him.

Betty's Tea Rooms oozed delightful aromas of fresh bread, coffee, and cake as I stepped in off the street and sat down at a table by the window. Soft piano music was playing upstairs as young table attendants, light on their feet, flitted between tables. Hungry, I ate two delicious warm cheese scones generously slathered in an excessive amount of butter, followed by an exquisite French Fancy washed down with coffee poured from a silver pot into a china cup. Cassie would have approved.

Reflecting on the three years since her passing, which seemed to have gone in a heartbeat, only now was I fulfilling a promise we made to one another on another lunch trip where we agreed we wouldn't give up on 'our jollies' if one of us died. But until now, that was precisely what I had done. I knew grief was a journey and not a place to stay, but right then, I wondered if I was moving through that journey. Collecting other people's stories that supported my experience for the past two years was exciting and distracting. But to what end?

Howard's Story

After returning home, not wanting to bother my new friend, I decided to hold off from contacting him. But something compelled me, and less than forty-eight hours later, I was staring at my computer screen excitedly, waiting for Howard to log in. He soon appeared, wearing a rainbow sweater, mustard dungarees, and a ready smile, sitting in a room with instant appeal.

Bohemian best describes it. A riot of pictures, some wonky against the daffodil yellow wall, indicated an affection for Warhol, Dali and Van Gogh. To his left stood a cluttered table on which yellowed sheet music, held down by a small bust of Nefertiti, threatened to spill onto the floor. Antique books, their bindings chipped and tattered, were stacked in piles throughout the room and in the corner, leaning against the wall behind a threadbare sofa on which two snoring chocolate labradors reclined, was a large black double bass.

"Hello Hannah, and how was York?"

We chatted about the merit of cheese scones and how much butter was considered excessive, train journeys, and York, until a loud screeching off in the near distance interrupted us and made me jump. Howard laughed at my surprise and told me that Barney, the African Grey parrot, was very vocal, and to ignore any insults I might hear. Apparently, he had picked them up when workers were doing some renovations to the house. The conversation was easy. I told him more about Cassie, our friendship, and the stories I was collecting.

After about fifteen minutes, Howard finally said, "Would you like to hear my story?"

"I would indeed," I replied, "but only if you are comfortable doing so."

"It's not a problem; I'll be honest with you, Hannah. I never intended to tell anyone about this, but as you were talking on the train, I knew I wanted you to hear it, and here we are. As you know, I come from a scientific background and worked in the petrochemical industry after I left university. I had no religious or spiritual beliefs, and when this event occurred I was a confirmed materialist with no thought or interest in an afterlife. I led a rather selfish existence; my only concern was acquiring wealth and promotion. Ruth, my wife, was a research assistant, too. We were young and successful, and believed our professional and private lives were mapped out before us.

"One night, over 30 years ago, along with our two young sons, we travelled overnight to our holiday home in Southern France. We were looking forward to a week of relaxation when a lorry ploughed into the nearside of our car at speed. Somehow, I was thrown from the vehicle, sustaining only a hand injury. Ruth and the boys were killed instantly.

"How I got there remains a mystery, but I found myself standing on the hard shoulder of the motorway, watching the emergency services heroically attempt to remove my family from the wreck. I saw my wife leave the car and approach me, yet I could also see her in the front passenger seat. Somehow, I knew she was dead.

"Always beautiful, she seemed even more lovely now as she glowed with soft brilliance. I heard her voice, though she never spoke, urging me to live. She said the boys would be OK with her. An indescribable feeling of love wrapped around me, and then, like pixels shattering, she disappeared before my eyes."

Shocked by the revelation and tragic circumstances of Howard's story, I muttered something inadequate about not continuing if it was too painful, but Howard held up his hand and smiled.

"It's OK, Hannah, none of us have the monopoly on grief. My tragedy is no greater than any other. I've lived with it for a long time, and I'm OK telling you. Besides, the story isn't finished yet."

Assuring Howard I was happy to continue listening, he went on.

"In a heartbeat, my world had been upended. Dark days followed, and I made terrible choices in the following months. I threw bottles of Jack Daniels down my throat and stuffed cocaine up my nose. Anything to numb the unrelenting pain. I was so far off my head daily, and I'm ashamed to say I don't even recall the funerals. I ate very little, and when I did, it was something grabbed from the corner shop chiller. Essentially, I had given up. I was so angry, hated the world, and struggled to see a future.

"One day, unexpectedly, my mother turned up at my house. I had been ignoring the phone, and she was naturally worried about me. She saw the booze bottles littering the house, piles of dirty washing in the bathroom, the messy stack of plastic food dishes, and even the drugs I hadn't bothered to hide away.

"I must have looked dreadful because she actually smelt my hair and asked how long it had been since I'd had a shower! After admitting I couldn't remember, without a word, and considering she's quite a small woman, she bodily hauled me out of the house, locked the door, put me in her car and drove me to her home in Wiltshire.

"It was what I needed. Almost zombie-like, I followed her instructions, and the first thing was to have a long bubble bath! Then she put me into bed. Mentally and physically drained, I slept excessively for days. Little by little, given the space I needed to heal, and with Mum's excellent cooking, long walks through the undulating chalk downlands, and the absence of drink or drugs, my physical health was restored. My emotional health would take longer.

"After about three months, Mum suggested bereavement counselling might help me. Appalled at the thought of meeting a stranger, let alone one that wanted to, as I wrongly thought, 'get inside my head', I vented my anger at her and told her to mind her own business, forgetting that she had also lost her grandchildren and a much-loved daughter-in-law. When the subject came up again a few weeks later, I agreed to try and found it helpful, but it didn't end the pain. Something more was needed, but I wasn't sure what that was."

Howard took a sip of coffee before going on. "The counsellor I had was a lovely lady, but couldn't or wouldn't discuss anything to do with an afterlife, which is what I wanted to talk about. In fact, when I broached the subject, she shut it down and suggested that perhaps I was unable to accept my loss, which was ridiculous, really. I fully accepted it; that's why I was having sessions with her. Now, of course, I understand that it wasn't in her remit to discuss what she termed 'religious beliefs.' Unfortunately, our meetings finally ended with me feeling that I was no further forward.

"Eventually, it took me about a year to start feeling anywhere near normal, whatever that is. I no longer cried as soon as my eyes opened in the morning, but it was slow progress. During my lowest moments, I found solace in recalling over and over again the crash's immediate aftermath.

"My logical brain told me the interaction with Ruth was impossible. Worried I'd lost reason, I told no one, not even my mum. How do you explain the inexplicable? Yet, I clung to those few seconds like a drowning man clings to a lifeline, regularly recalling them for comfort.

"Unable to return to our former home, my mother arranged for it to be sold, and I eventually moved here. I resigned from my post in the petrochemical industry, and it was the best thing I could have done. I began a new career with a company concerned with saving the planet rather than destroying it. Gradually, my whole worldview began to shift. I had learned a hard lesson about what's really valuable in this life. I regretted the hugs I didn't give, the kisses for our children I didn't have time for in my pursuit of status and money.

"Apart from work, I became a hermit, and reading was what filled my life; devouring everything about spiritualism, mediumship, psychics, you name it, I read about it, finding reassurance in discovering that historically, many eminent scientists, including Einstein, had a more than passing interest in the subject.

"The books inspired me, but proving I hadn't hallucinated that night became a personal imperative. I so wanted it to be real, and the scientist in me screamed, "Prove it!" To that end, I sought out the services of a number of mediums in an attempt to find that one bit of evidence that was so specific that only Ruth and I knew about it. That was the gold standard I sought, but I would have to wait to get it."

Howard paused, took a mouthful of coffee from his Darth Vader mug, smiled, and said, "It was about ten years after the accident when, suddenly, life got better. I hadn't given up looking for that gold standard, and my interest in mediumship hadn't waned when, on an unexpected overnight stopover in Glasgow, I found what I was waiting for.

"A few streets from where I was staying, I had noticed an event advertised as I passed by a venue earlier in the day. A demonstration of mediumship was taking place there that night. I'd never heard of the medium, and the alternative was watching TV in my hotel room with a takeaway so, always hopeful but expecting nothing, I got to the venue early and settled into my seat.

"The event was well attended, and the medium was the young Scottish fellow whose book you were reading on the train. About halfway through, he got a link, which I knew was for me. Once I had claimed it, the medium expressly referred to a gift I had given Ruth on our honeymoon. He even correctly named the unique place I had given it to her, something no one else knew about. That's what I had been waiting for! I happily took the message, but there was more. He confirmed I'd seen her and that she had spoken to me after the accident. Either this man was telepathic and could read my memory (an impressive feat in itself), or he was receiving that information from the only other person who knew about those things, my wife. I chose to believe the latter."

Howard stopped talking. A smile crossed his face as he recalled the moment before continuing his story. "I left the small hall, walking on air. Outside, rain was falling, the wet street sparkled and shimmered in the glow of the street lamps, and I felt a lightness of heart that had been absent for too long. Walking alone through the unfamiliar streets, pedestrians huddled under umbrellas moved quickly through the drizzle. I relished the gentle rain mingling with my happy tears. The warm glow and tempting smell of a tiny fish and chip shop drew me to its doors. With supper ordered, I went outside to wait. Looking up at the stars, I said a prayer of thanks to whoever had made that night possible.

"Later, sitting on the edge of a hotel bed somewhere in central Glasgow, understanding finally dawned. Ruth was clever. She knew me so well. She had given me the gift of life the night she died. I saw and heard her in spirit form because, undoubtedly, I would not have continued living without that. She also knew my analytical mind wouldn't allow me to accept what had happened after the crash without question and that I would want to make sense of it. My desire to find out would keep me going. Indeed, those brief seconds we shared had sustained me until a young medium could give me the confirmation I had sought for so long.

"My life with Ruth didn't end the night of the accident, Hannah; it was merely interrupted for a while. That medium's message showed me that when it's my time, we will be reunited. I'm convinced of that. Knowing there is no death has allowed me to really live. Now, my life is more prosperous in ways I could once never have anticipated."

I stared at this man, a stranger to me until a few days ago, who had shared this remarkable story without any sign of self-pity. In the brief silence that followed, I felt awkward and at a loss how to respond. What should I say now?

I heard myself saying, "Wow. That's a hell of a story, I really don't know what to say other than thank you for sharing it with me."

As if on cue, one of the labradors, who until now had been fast asleep, popped its head up and looked toward Howard. Sliding lazily off the sofa, the dog made its way over to where he sat, its claws clicking on the wooden floor. The other dog yawned deeply, sat up, and stretched before joining him. Digger and Dave were formally introduced, and Howard informed me it was time for their walk and that he'd have to go. I thanked him for his time, and finally, as we were about to log off, he asked what I would do with his story.

"I'll keep it safe with the others; don't worry, no one has access to them," I assured him.

A quizzical look passed over his face.

"Oh, really? I'm sorry, I misunderstood. I thought you were collecting them to publish them somewhere."

"No, that hadn't occurred to me. I just enjoy reading them. It wasn't my intention to do anything with them. I'm sorry if that's what you thought was happening?"

Howard laughed. "My mistake for assuming."

"I'm kinda protective of the stories," I admitted. "They are so deeply personal and, like yours, kindly given to me in confidence; I must be tender with them. The world is full of naysayers who are quick to rubbish people's experiences. I imagine you'd feel pretty shitty if someone did that to your story?"

"Agreed! But how many people might take comfort from them? During my dark days, I would have welcomed stories like those you are collecting, but hey, that's just my thoughts... Look, I really have to go; Dave is dancing and Digger really needs to pee. Let's keep in touch."

Promising we would, the meeting ended.

Timely Interventions

Howard's story showed me that even in the face of tragedy, as hard as it might be, we should strive to continue living. The death of a loved one is not the end of our lives. Seeing Ruth undoubtedly helped him and his story left me with a lot to think about. Over the following weeks, I encountered people who had interesting stories to tell about how spirit interaction using third parties can affect someone's thinking or behaviour, as the following story from Helen shows:

"During my early twenties, I shared an old Victorian house with fellow students I attended college with. Early one morning, around 5am, I awoke suddenly, and a bathroom trip was needed. Upon returning to bed half asleep, I glanced at the clock and noted it would be another hour or so before the alarm went off. I sat on the bed and swung my feet around. At the end of the bed was a friend, Pat, who had been killed on his motorbike a few weeks earlier when a car pulled out in front of him. Both he and his pillion passenger had died instantly.

"Although startled, I wasn't afraid, and bizarrely, there was no thought that this was strange. It all happened so quickly. I blurted out "What did you think when you realised you were dead?"

"A picture came into my head of him standing beside the road, looking confused, wondering what had just happened. Then I heard, "It wasn't meant to be like this," and then,

"It's her I feel sorry for."

"The picture changed to that of his partner, Sonya. Then it was gone, and I was staring into space.

"It was over in a flash, and it didn't occur to me that I had just had a psychic experience. Almost immediately, my head told me I had 'just imagined' what had happened; I was drowsy after all. Maybe I was dreaming?

"I lay back down and quickly went to sleep. When the alarm woke me an hour later, I immediately felt the compulsion to tell Sonya what had happened—a compulsion I ignored at first.

"At college, I spoke about what had happened with a few mutual friends. One looked at me horrified and demanded I never mention it again. I think she thought I was a nutter. In fact, everyone agreed it would be wrong to say anything, as it could upset Sonya.

"I failed to see how much more upset she could be than she was at the moment. She was struggling to cope with grief and a new baby, born within days of Pat's death. The old adage 'If in doubt, don't!' rang in my ears. I was beginning to think I had made the whole thing up. What right did I have to impose on her what I was starting to believe might be my imagination?

"But the nagging compulsion to call her wouldn't go away. It was like a churning in the middle of my stomach, and it increased as the day wore on.

"As it was a Friday, after a week of lectures, like many of my friends, I was looking forward to getting as drunk as possible, hitting a club, and nursing a hangover for the weekend. But that night would be different.

"Our usual sizeable group turned out to be just two of us. The pub was crowded and noisy, and the only seats available were opposite an oversized wall clock. I ended up staring at the clock, sipping lemonade when my first drink had uncharacteristically made me retch, and trying to hear what my companion, who couldn't have been less impressed, was saying. The night had all the hallmarks of being a total disaster as I sat there distracted by the growing thought that I had a phone call to make. The gnawing feeling in my stomach became a tight knot, and my eyes kept being dragged back to the clock.

"As I look back over the years, I don't know what finally made me decide to phone Sonya, but I did. Mobile phones had yet to be invented, and a public telephone in a noisy pub really wasn't the place to make a sensitive call. Around ten o'clock, I finally threw in the towel, made my excuses about feeling a bit 'dodgy', and, with my stomach still churning, headed for home.

"I rang Sonya's number on the house phone as soon as I got in. I wasn't feeling brave, and a part of me wanted her to not answer because I was feeling pretty silly. I had already decided that if she didn't answer by the fifth ring, it was a sign that I shouldn't do this. To my horror, She picked up on the second, and I blurted out, "I've seen Pat."

"I went on and told her what had happened and that he looked well and, in particular, he had all his front teeth he'd lost a couple of years before when he fell over while drunk.

As I talked to her, I became aware that the churning in my stomach had stopped.

"We met up the following day, and she wanted to hear every tiny detail of what I had witnessed in those few seconds in my bedroom. But more was needed. I suggested we visit the local Spiritualist church. As it was Saturday, there was an evening of clairvoyance happening. Hoping for the best, we made our way there, understanding that there was no guarantee of receiving a message.

"The little church had a small platform, and I would have gotten up there next to the medium if I could have. I wanted her to notice us. We sat right at the front. The woman must have thought me quite mad as I fixed my unblinking gaze on her, willing her to bring a message through. At that time, I didn't fully understand how mediumship worked. Perhaps I felt that staring at her like a mad person was conducive to good communication, but desperate times need desperate acts. Frustratingly, nothing came.

"Sonya tried to smile, but her disappointment was palpable. Grasping at straws without anything else to say that would help her, I made some pathetic comment about it "not being the right time yet." Just then, as we made our way to the exit, I saw one of the church elders approaching.

"She smiled at us and, looking at Sonya, said. "My dear, would you like to come with me? I'm aware that someone from spirit wants to talk to you."

"I waited outside, relieved that Sonya was getting some help. She had been gone a long time, and when she came out of the church, she was smiling. Her beloved Pat had come through, and his message was one of hope.

"It was only years later, when talking to her one day that I came to fully understand the urgency I had experienced to call her. Her grief seemed too deep to bear, and she had planned to commit suicide the night I called. The call and subsequent message she got at church didn't end her grief journey, but it stopped a course of action that would have been truly tragic."

The compulsion that made Helen make the phone call in spite of her own misgivings couldn't be ignored. Likewise, the outcome of our next story was driven by Sandra, a young mother who, in spite of the advice given by those around her, chose instead to listen to a disembodied voice she was hearing that told her that advice was wrong.

I met Sandra one weekend at a metaphysical convention where she was tutoring some classes. Thinking I recognised her, I found myself constantly looking across to where she was. At coffee time, we began chatting. I liked her immediately and told her about the stories I was collecting. When she said she had one I might be interested in, we arranged to hook up online when the convention was over.

Sandra was 21 when she had her first daughter, Paula. The baby was a good weight, and both mother and baby were well. After receiving all the checks that the newborn babies needed, they left the hospital. They went to stay with Sandra's mother in Hawick.

All appeared well for a while. However, on the day Sandra stopped feeding naturally, following the advice of a healthcare professional, things changed. The wee baby, unsettled by the switch, wouldn't feed from the bottle. The following morning, feeling concerned, she naturally sought the advice of her mum, who, being a mother of ten herself and with the wisdom that affords women of that experience, advised Sandra that it was natural for a baby changing to being bottle-fed to be restless for a day or two, and not to worry. It did little to ease Sandra's feeling that all was not well.

At about 8am, Sandra heard a male voice insisting that her baby wasn't okay. She began repeatedly hearing 'She's sick, she's sick'. By lunchtime, the voice had grown more insistent, telling Sandra her daughter needed to see a doctor.

Although the baby didn't appear ill, Sandra insisted that her mother call the doctor. Witnessing Sandra's anxious behaviour, her mother, who had no phone in the house, went to a neighbour's house and made the call.

The doctor duly attended later that day. He thoroughly checked the baby and found nothing wrong with her. He agreed with Sandra's mum that babies can take a couple of days to settle when coming off of the breast, and advised Sandra to give it a day or two.

As he went to leave, Sandra heard the voice again. It was loud and clear, and the tone was solid and urgent. 'Don't let him go!' it insisted. Sandra implored the doctor to stay, but as he left the house, the voice again demanded, 'Don't let him go!' Sandra ran after him, pulling on the arm of his coat, insisting the baby was unwell, urging him to return.

Perhaps the sight of a distressed young mother pleading

with him made the doctor return to the house. He looked at the baby again and lifted her from her moses basket. He turned to Sandra and said he was sending her to the local hospital for a check-up. Sandra's mother later admitted that the doctor had confided to her that he wasn't worried about the baby at that point. His decision to send her to the hospital was made to settle Sandra's mind.

But that situation rapidly changed.

The doctor went to the neighbours and called an ambulance. It took only minutes, but on his return to the house, he glanced into the Moses basket, picked up the baby, began studying the child intently, then looked up and said, "This baby is seriously ill, and she needs to go to the hospital immediately!"

The ambulance arrived quickly and the paramedics were told the gravity of the situation and instructed to use blue lights. The baby was taken to Peel Hospital, a former health facility used for military casualties during the war, which was set within a forested part of the Scottish Borders.

Due to the hospital's remote location, the phone connection was often poor and affected by high winds. That day, it was down, so the hospital was unprepared for a highly sick baby now en route to them. On arrival at the hospital's gates, the paediatrician who would later treat Paula was leaving for the weekend. Fortunately, the ambulance bringing the baby in barred her way.

The paediatrician, seeing the baby, understood the gravity of the situation, and Paula was rushed into intensive care. By now, she was convulsing. Sandra was told that her baby was suffering from bacterial meningitis. This often fatal infection affects the membranes that line the brain and spinal cord and requires urgent medical treatment. Usually, the baby would be transferred to Edinburgh Hospital, where better facilities existed. Still, Sandra was told that the baby was too poorly and it was unlikely she would survive the journey.

The police took Paula's blood to Edinburgh to confirm the diagnosis. She was fitting continuously as her body became overwhelmed by the infection. For two days and nights, the doctors fought to save her. A minister was called to baptise the baby, and Sandra was given the worst news, her baby was dying. The doctors were at a loss for what to do. Antibiotics appeared to have no effect. Paula's little head swelled as the infection raged on, forcing her eyes to bulge from their sockets.

In despair, Sandra suddenly heard the same male voice that had urged her to get help, only this time it told her that her baby was safe, she would be fine, and that she was out of the woods now.

Sandra said that the voice brought a calmness that washed over her. She knew to trust it. The voice repeated his words, 'She's fine, she's out of the woods now,' Sandra knew she would survive even though Paula's condition still appeared critical and the Doctors had not given any sign that recovery was even possible.

There appeared to be no hope for the baby, and Sandra was offered sedation to help her cope with what was coming. An offer she happily refused, knowing her baby would be okay. She was so confident in her voice that she gave the good news to her parents when they arrived at the hospital. Yet when her mother spoke to the doctors privately, they swiftly denied that was the case and suggested that perhaps Sandra was denying the inevitable. They insisted the situation was hopeless and Sandra's mother should do her best to prepare her daughter for losing her child.

On the third morning, Paula showed no discernable improvement. Yet Sandra was unconcerned; the voice continued telling her, "She's fine." Sandra happily went for a shower, and on her way to her daughter's room afterwards heard laughter coming from inside. On the way in, she met the doctor, who urged her to hurry because "something unbelievable has happened!"

Little Paula was indeed 'out of the woods'. Her vital signs were returning to normal. She had turned a corner, and everything indicated that she would make a recovery. The doctors were still concerned. Bacterial meningitis in babies so young can leave severe long-term problems. All the tests showed she could see and hear okay, and the hydrocephalus causing her head to swell was draining away.

Once fully well, Paula and Sandra returned home. On her daughter's first birthday, Sandra wrote to the hospital staff and sent a picture of her healthy little girl to thank those who had worked so hard to save her. Later, she received a letter, which she still has, from the paediatrician involved with Paula's recovery, saying Paula was 'the sickest baby she had ever cared for'.

Little Paula is now a mum of two, and Sandra, a doting grandmother. The infection that caused doctors so much worry left some mild physical symptoms but nothing that has stopped her from enjoying life to the full.

To this day, Sandra doesn't know whose voice she heard. She had never heard it before and hasn't heard it since. Her belief and trust in it compelled her to disregard the advice of her mother and doctor, and to insist action was taken. Had she not, the outcome may have been very different.

Tails of the Unexpected

Helen and Sandra's stories provide robust evidence that something outside of our normal perception can, when necessary, get involved in the lives of those needing help. I looked forward to discussing this with Howard when I saw him next.

In the meantime, Herbie died quickly and unexpectedly late one night. He was loved by everyone and was greatly missed. Rescued from an unpleasant situation, he came into my life the year before Cassie died and was a great source of comfort through the early days of the grief journey.

Within a couple of days, a visitor to my house saw him in the garden. I wasn't surprised; I knew that sightings of companion animals are often witnessed after they have passed away. In fact, there were a good number of such stories in my collection.

Interestingly, I discovered that regardless of personal beliefs in an afterlife, people were only too happy to discuss seeing their treasured pet. Reece was a nonbeliever until his beloved Bono passed from this life at the Summer Solstice 2022.

Bono's food and water bowls were metal dishes on raised

feeders. To alert the family that he was hungry, Bono had learned to lick the bowl's side, raising it up so it would clank back down. Soon after Bono passed, Reece was working from home and went downstairs to make some lunch. He was alone, his wife was at work, and the kids were at school; the house was silent until, lo and behold, Bono's bowl started clanking.

Another story I received was from Ann, about the death of her eight-year-old Golden Retriever, Bonnie. This heartwarming story speaks volumes about the love we share with our four-legged friends but, perhaps most importantly, how, like us, their spirit survives.

"Bonnie was very much loved by the whole family. She would settle down on the front lawn, atop a hill overlooking a public footpath and the rest of the close. She'd sit there like the Queen of Sheba, looking down on the world until she was ready to woof for the door to be opened.

"One Christmas, I noticed a swelling on her tummy when she was lolling in front of the TV. As soon as we could, we took her to the vet, who x-rayed her and said her spleen was swollen. Not sure about the cause, she booked her in for an exploratory operation a couple of days later.

"We took her on Friday teatime; surgery was scheduled for that evening, and the vet said she would be OK to come home on Saturday teatime. However, on Saturday morning, we had a call to say that she was too poorly to go home, it would now be Sunday or Monday.

"On a whim, I suggested the family visit the vet. Bonnie was groggy, but as soon as she saw us, she tried in vain to haul herself up, and our son climbed into the cage to cuddle her instead. The vet said her spleen had been hugely swollen, but she didn't know why because there was no sign of anything wrong with the liver, which would be the usual suspect, so she'd do some further tests. We said goodbye, planning on picking her up on Sunday.

"That night, just before 3 a.m., I awoke from a deep, sound sleep into an unusual state of high alert. Honestly, it is hard to describe, but I knew something felt very wrong. I listened in silence.

"I crept out of bed (we had been burgled in the past while we were all at home, so I was taking precautions) and onto the landing into our son's room. He was sound asleep. I went into our daughter's room; she was fast asleep, too. I checked the spare room and the main bathroom and returned to our room. My husband was still sleeping. I even checked the en-suite and airing cupboard; I felt so wired.

"Downstairs, I put all the lights on and checked the dining room, the downstairs cupboard, the breakfast bar in the kitchen, the back lobby, the downstairs loo, and even Bonnie's bed. Nothing, just this inexplicable state of high alert.

"I went back to bed but couldn't settle. It was a very bright, frosty, moonlit night. I got up and opened our front window wide and leaned out, listening, looking for something, but I didn't know what— when I recognised a sound that was so familiar to me. It was the sound Bonnie made when she crossed the front lawn, pausing as she always did before trotting down the slope and past the oak tree at the bottom. The crisp frost made the sound perfectly audible in the silence, but nothing was visible in the clear cold night. I went back to bed, thinking how odd it was.

"At 8:00 o'clock the following day, the vet called. When I heard her voice, I knew what she was going to say, and I even knew what time our Bonnie had slipped away, ten to three. I had to wake the children to tell them the news, and the only thing I could say to help was that she had come to say goodbye.

"Our son was particularly devastated. I kept him off school the next day because he was so upset. Many weeks later, he came home and told me something had happened in his maths class. He had been suddenly filled with the knowledge that Bonnie had found wherever she was looking for and had gone home."

An entire book could be written about animals interacting with humans after their passing. The grief we feel when they leave us is in no way less because they have fur or feathers. Their love for us and ours for them is beyond doubt. When the time comes for them to leave us, it can be heartbreaking, especially if we have to make the decision that all animal guardians fear – to help them pass.

Orla was faced with making that hard decision when her 13-year-old Akita Staffy cross, Buster, developed anal cancer.

Buster was rescued when he was three. Much loved by the family, he had been showing signs of old age - not being able to get upstairs anymore without the help of a human, not wanting to play, and sleeping a lot. Then it was noticed that something was growing out of his butt.

Following a biopsy, the vet gave the worst news possible: it was cancer, it had its own blood supply, was aggressive, and was growing from the inside outwards. The results were sent to a canine cancer specialist and a laboratory in Cambridge for further testing, and both confirmed the diagnosis.

The vet suggested that surgery followed by chemotherapy was possible, but the results couldn't be guaranteed. The family could have Buster put to sleep immediately, or let nature take its course. Buster went home with Orla and her husband while they decided what would be best for their doggy friend.

Usually cheerful, Orla was sad and down when she told me what was happening. Conflicted, she didn't know what course of action to take. We talked about spiritual healing and how it has been used to bring about remarkable improvements in humans and animals alike. We both shared a belief that healing comes in on a vibration of love and discussed how her love for him might help Buster and that by stroking him, she was giving him healing. She agreed it was the way to go but looked sad as she left.

Four nights later, she was back at mine all smiles. Unbelievably, the tumour had gone! Orla's daughter noticed it had disappeared. It hadn't been chewed off or dropped off; the area was as clear as if nothing had ever been there. The vets were flabbergasted.

Of course, everyone was happy at this turn of events. But there was something else. It seemed as if Buster had been given a new lease of life. He was once again running up and down the stairs on his own and playing like a young dog.

A French Connection

One evening, my text alert went off. It was Howard. "Fancy hooking up for a chat?"

There was much I wanted to discuss with him, and I quickly replied, "Yeah, I'm free now; let me grab a coffee first."

Five minutes later, sitting on Zoom, Howard logged in, and I was met with a cheery, "Hey how are you?"

Howard was smiling at me from the screen. We exchanged pleasantries, and I told him about Herbie's passing and the stories from Ann and Reece. We shared some doggy experiences, and he told me he was a couple of days away from flying to Tokyo for work, and that his mum would be looking after Digger and Dave. We were discussing the merits of Japanese food when he said, "So you aren't going to publish your stories?"

"Wow, nice pivot from Udon noodles and Sushi. I'm impressed!" I exclaimed, "Yeah, I've considered it and taken on board what you said, but I have reservations".

"Such as?"

"Not being believed for a start. The world is too quick to trash other people's experiences; some stories sound far out."

"But you believe them?"

"Absolutely. I know they come from credible people with no agenda other than sharing their experiences with me. Why would they make them up?"

"Then stand by them and consider sharing them; they could help people."

"I'm not trying to prove anything here," I interrupted.

Howard raised an eyebrow and smiled before continuing. "Are you absolutely sure about that? Aren't you trying to prove something, at least to yourself?"

"Um, yes, yes, I am, I guess."

"So..."

"Where are you going with this Howard?"

"Well, here's the thing, Hannah. I get it; I really do. Like me, you experienced something remarkable, and like me, you feel compelled to prove to yourself that what you saw wasn't a hallucination. It's important to you. You've collected these stories because they support what you saw, but I wonder if you are fearful because you still think you might have imagined it all."

"You sound like a psychologist," I smiled. "But you are right. It is important to me to have no doubt. I guess years of indoctrination have made me more sceptical than I care to admit."

"I'm sorry, Hannah. I don't mean to sound like a shrink. I was fearful of telling anybody, too, that is, until I met you.

But if you did consider publishing from what you've told me thus far, your own experience and the stories from others are anecdotal and, whilst compelling, prove nothing, sadly. If you are worried about the naysayers trashing them, consider widening your research to include events that can be validated by third parties."

"Is that the scientist speaking?" I laughed

"Absolutely it is. And you will find your what you are looking for, of that I'm sure - and when you do, share it. Imagine if Fleming hadn't shared his discovery of penicillin."

"That's a good point, but it's a tall order. OK, I'll give it some more thought."

A loud beeping interrupted our chat, followed by "Caution, this vehicle is reversing".

I looked at Howard, who was laughing.

"What is that? It's so loud!" I asked.

"Barney has learned to imitate a vehicle motion alarm. I don't know how. Clever, isn't he? It's new, and he uses it when I'm not paying him any attention."

The interruption halted the conversation as a stream of obscenities filled the air, and his incessant squawking made it impossible to carry on. After wishing Howard well for the upcoming trip, and with a lot to think about, I logged off and headed for the coffee machine in the kitchen.

Sipping the creamy latte, I leaned back in my chair, mulling over our discussion. Howard had a way of making me think about stuff, and he was right. Why was it necessary to prove anything? I was convinced I'd seen Cassie; wasn't that enough? Obviously not, because a nagging thought constantly troubled me: what if I was wrong?

Realisation dawned. It was my objectivity, I doubted. The stories were a supportive comfort blanket when doubt crept in. Like Howard, I had to find the proof for myself. Unsure what that might look like, something told me that doubt would melt away when it finally came.

Within days, I stumbled upon an article about a retreat in France where, according to the account, manifestations via Physical Mediumship of Native American spirits were regularly occurring at séances. Furthermore, the hosts welcomed open-minded spiritual seekers to attend these séances. The article said that other phenomena would be witnessed, including transfiguration and ectoplasmic hands, which some visitors were invited to touch.

Dialogue with the Spirit of John Campbell Sloan, a humble Glasgow medium, via direct voice mediumship, was also possible within the beautiful setting of a vintage French farmhouse. The three-day stay included a complimentary French evening meal upon arrival, followed by a séance with two more on consecutive nights. Was this where the proof I sought might be had? I knew that the circle in which I sat each week would be interested in the article, too.

Our circle had started accidentally years before and grew from a group of friends, with a mutual interest in the paranormal, meeting every week for coffee cake and 'spook night' where we discussed and exchanged books, watched films, tried to meditate and sometimes had a go at psychometry which much to our surprise yielded some exciting results.

Over the years, we had acquired a library of old esoteric books in which séances such as those now advertised in France were described. We knew what to expect, and we all wanted to see it, so with the promise of witnessing actual spirits walking around the séance room and talking to us, we all jumped at the chance to go.

Shenanigans in the Séance Room

Three months later, our circle members, Matty, Orla, Gertie, Enya, and I boarded a flight to the Languedoc region of France. We were joined by another friend, Dorcas. After a short flight and speedy disembarkation at the tiny Carcassonne airport, we picked up our rental car.

Matty, using the lame excuse that being a passenger made him car sick, swiftly insisted he drive. Enya maintained she could only sit in the front seat because she was pregnant and needed the room. When someone pointed out that being six weeks pregnant really didn't justify needing a roomier seat, she appeared to have developed selective hearing and cheerfully ignored us. In high spirits, the rest of us, full of anticipation, squeezed into the back of the car and headed out into the medieval landscape.

This delightful part of France has the appearance and feel of real age. We travelled through countryside dotted with 13th Century castles, lush vineyards, and sleepy villages and passed fields of cheerful sunflowers, their brilliant butter-yellow petals turned to face the sun.

A stop at the irresistibly charming town of Mirepoix to buy supplies enchanted us. We walked on uneven cobblestones through old streets with their vibrant, multicoloured, half-timbered houses. Adorned with carved grotesques, the quaint shops and cafes spilt shadows and promises of delicious foods into the busy, narrow lanes. Knowing a welcome meal awaited us, we agreed to return there to eat when we had more time.

The long but agreeable drive took us into rural France's heart, and we finally arrived at Hameau Sanctuaire de Raphael, a stunning faded pink vintage farmhouse. It was nestled at the end of a long straight road in a tiny hamlet with four further buildings, surrounded by olive trees and rolling hills.

Battered by time, blue window shutters opened against pink peeling walls where ripe grapes hugged a meandering trellis. We pulled onto the gravel courtyard. There, sitting on faded wooden chairs under trailing Kiwi vines, our hosts were waiting for us.

Don and husband Melvin were friendly, open and welcoming. They showed us around the extensive garden and meditation area. We politely ignored the algae floating like a fringe several inches from the side of the swimming pool on which a frog was sitting. After all, we were there for séances, not swimming.

Inside our apartment, the rustic décor was undoubtedly authentic. The acrid smell of recently extinguished embers pervaded the room, and cobwebs covered the exposed stone and brickwork. A majestic oak fireplace commanded the living area; its antique grate, elevated by wrought iron scrolling, stood proudly above a pyramid of grey ash. Above, heavily patinated copper pots hung from ceiling hooks that were overlaid with a sooty curtain of cobwebs.

Grey dust coated the window ledges and furniture, and horrifyingly, in the kitchen area, draped above the sizeable wooden farmhouse table, a giant spider sat in the centre of an impressive web, waiting for unsuspecting victims.

Upon seeing this, Matty released a shrill scream and shot up the stairs with Gertie uttering a string of expletives close behind him. The rest of us backed away and took refuge behind the tattered sofas dotted about the large room.

Orla, the practical one of the group, ran outside, returning quickly with a pleasant man called Steve, who bravely grasped the offending arachnid and took it into the garden. The friendly man was from Yorkshire and chatted with us briefly. After informing us that it was the third giant spider he'd removed from the apartments since his arrival, which reassured no one, he went on to tell us the séance was at 7.30pm. Enya mentioned the welcome meal and asked what time that would be. His look was quizzical, "What meal? I'm not aware of anything happening," he said before leaving us to settle in.

We looked at each other and began laughing. As Gertie eloquently put it, "It's a bit grim, isn't it?" It was undoubtedly different from what we expected. To our relief, the bedrooms appeared sparse but clean, with thankfully no cobwebs. Enya complained she was hungry, and with no sign of the promised welcome meal, we tore into the bread, cheeses, ham and chocolate our stop at Mirepoix had yielded.

Later, we explored the tiny hamlet and introduced ourselves

to the other séance attendees, chatting around the pool. We were a mixed lot: us from the UK, several people from different European countries including Holland and Germany, two doctors from the USA, a publisher who lived in Lilydale, New York, and one man who had flown in from Queensland just for this event, which he reliably informed us was going to be amazing.

Excited and comfortable, we sat and listened as stories of previous séances were related. After we admitted that this was our first time, our fellow attendees jostled with one another to show how much experience they had. Melvin and Don's names flitted in and out of the conversation, accompanied by much praise, until the assembly ran out of superlatives to describe them. We were obviously in good hands.

Melvin appeared from what we later learned was the séance room. He informed us that the sitting would start in half an hour and we could pay the fee to Don.

Gertie hissed quietly at me, "What fee?"

"I haven't a clue," I hissed back.

Convinced the advert had said séances were included in the price and worried that I had got it wrong, I jumped up and headed for the apartment. A quick rifle through my phone revealed the advert and booking form, clearly stating that the price covered séances too. Gertie was right behind me, and I turned and showed her. She read it and passed the phone to Enya and Orla, who had joined us.

"I need to go and see them," I said, "and ask what the score is; this clearly states that the price includes séances."

"Yeah, ask about the meal while you are there," Enya said. "I'm still hungry."

Gertie followed me from the apartment, and we found Don in the garden pruning roses. After an exchange of pleasantries, I asked, "Have we got to pay for attending the séance this evening?'

"Yes, is there a problem?"

"I think so, your advert says that séances are included in the price."

"Normally, that would be correct, but a well-known international medium, Carron Naylor, is here, and so we apply a surcharge of £50 each to cover her travelling costs from America. You won't want to miss her. Of course, if you prefer not to come..."

"It might be a good idea to let attendees know this surcharge applies before they arrive," I retorted quickly. "Will she be doing the séances all weekend?"

My tone of voice suggested I wasn't happy.

"Yes, that's why she is here."

"So it's £50 per person for each one this weekend?"

"Yes," was his quick reply.

Feeling slightly annoyed, I thanked him, completely

forgetting about the meal. With Gertie swearing softly under her breath, I returned to the apartment to impart the news to the others, who were equally unimpressed with this turn of events.

A hurried discussion ensued. We had come all this way and didn't want to miss anything. What was the alternative? Sit in the apartment and moan about missing a great opportunity, or bite the bullet and pay?

We paid.

Our former high spirits were slightly dimmed; nonetheless, we were still full of anticipation and expectation as we approached the séance room. The room was long with low ceilings; it felt cold and had the musty smell that damp, unused, old buildings sometimes have. It was like all the séance rooms we had ever read about. Chairs lined the black windowless walls in a horseshoe shape, and a sturdy armchair sat within a curtained cabinet positioned so all attendees could see it clearly.

Melvin instructed us to remove anything with a reflective surface, including spectacles and jewellery, explaining that the metal could burn us if ectoplasm was produced. After he showed us our seats, he instructed us not to move from them during the séance. Soft music was playing from a device on a small table.

A few moments later, Don came into the room accompanied by a small, thin woman in her fifties whom we hadn't seen until then and introduced her as Carron, the medium for the evening. The heavy smell of Honeysuckle accompanied her arrival, cutting through the stale air and wafting around the room. It was overpowering, and Enya, sitting on my left, complained that it made her feel nauseous.

Don informed us that the evening's séance would include profound trance philosophy, transfiguration, and, if we were lucky, direct voice communication and production of ectoplasm. The atmosphere was electric as the twenty-plus attendees chatted excitedly, waiting for the event to start.

Carron went and sat in the sturdy chair. The music stopped, and the lights dimmed. Melvin invited the attendee from Queensland to step up and confirm that the cable ties he was now using to attach Carron's arms to the chair arms were tight and that she was anchored into the chair. Queensland man confirmed this was the case.

Don pulled the curtains shut, and a small red light went on above the curtained-off area; the lights further dimmed until we were sitting in complete blackness; music briefly played, and the curtains were pulled back, the red light allowing everyone in the room to see the medium sitting with her eyes shut.

Melvin then announced, "The séance will now begin."

Suddenly, loud, heavy music blasted into the room. It was uncomfortable and disorienting and far removed from the uplifting, happy music we had read was expected at séances. It continued for several minutes, reaching a violent crescendo before stopping suddenly.

Carron grasped the arms of the chair and began making guttural noises. Melvin's voice came from the blackness. He informed us that Carron would now demonstrate transfiguration and profound philosophy. He urged us to keep watching her as we would recognise the faces she would bring through.

The profound philosophy went on for about fifteen minutes and left me confused. It was in a language unknown to me. In fact, it sounded like gobbledegook. There wasn't one recognisable syllable in it. Other sitters' comments of "Wow, thank you, spirit" and "That's remarkable" left me wondering if the loud music had affected my perception. The only thing I found remarkable was that those sitters were hearing something completely different from me.

Eager voices called from the dark that they saw their loved one's faces transfiguring over the medium's face. One female voice claimed to have seen Bob Marley. The lighting was low, and I knew that could transform how we perceive things, so I observed closely, seeing what looked like Carron gurning her face. This continued for about ten minutes before she slumped in the chair, apparently exhausted.

Eventually, we were told that direct voice mediumship would now be attempted. Carron needed the curtains closed and the red light turned off for that. We were treated to more loud music as we sat for a few minutes until it abruptly stopped, and a diminutive Scottish male voice was heard.

"Is there anyone there?"

"Is there anyone there?" the soft voice repeated.

"I thought that's what we were supposed to say," sniggered Gertie on my right-hand side.

Melvin's voice informed us that this was John Campbell Sloane communicating.

My heart was racing; we were about to hear something only a few people had ever witnessed. I squeezed Enya and Gertie's hands and got a comforting squeeze in response.

The voice called out a name, and I felt Gertie nudge me. She and I knew the name being called, but it wasn't the name of a real person. It was the assumed name a friend used on an internet site. She and I shared an email address for admin purposes on that site, and the address contained the unique name now being called.

My heart sank as I realised It was from the email that I had used to return the booking form to Melvin before our arrival.

Then, from just behind my left ear, I heard the voice from the riverbank.

"This is not real."

Intense disappointment washed over me. When no one responded to the name being called, the performance continued, but I had little interest in it. The voice from the riverbank was, I knew, trustworthy, but the same couldn't be said about the voice claiming to be John Sloane. Surely, Spirit would never make the mistake of calling someone by a made-up name that belonged essentially to nobody?

Gertie was first back to our apartment after the séance finished. I could tell by her walking speed that she wasn't happy. She headed for the kitchen and busied herself, putting the kettle on and preparing coffee cups. The rest of us trailed in and sat quietly deflated around the large farmhouse table.

"Well, what did you think?" Gertie said as we sat down.

We all began to talk at once. Dorcas was convinced she had seen her mother's face during the transfiguration. Still, the rest of us were concerned what we were seeing wasn't what it was purported to be. I expressed my misgivings over the wrong name being called and hearing, "This is not real."

None of us understood anything said during the trance philosophy and agreed it sounded like gibberish. Ever the optimist, Dorcas suggested it could be a long-forgotten ancient tongue, like Latin, that no one ever used now. To which Gertie quickly retorted, "What the hell would the point be in using a language no one can understand if philosophy is to teach or enlighten?"

We all agreed it was a fair point and that, most confusingly, the other attendees seemed to see and hear things we couldn't. Perplexed, we talked long into the night and concluded that something seemed amiss.

The following morning, hungry, we set off early and found a shop where we loaded up with pasta, bread, cheese, ham, croissants and pan au chocolate. We returned to the farmhouse and, throughout the day, chatted with the other attendees about the night before. They appeared happy, and it was clear they had no misgivings about the event.

Carron made a brief appearance as we sat in the sun around the pool. She informed us that her guide had told her that this evening's séance would include the production of ectoplasm and the manifestation of a spirit hand. Looking around the group, her eyes settled on Orla.

"And you are a lucky lady." She said, pointing at Orla.

Orla's eyes were wide.

Carron went on. "My guide has spoken," she paused dramatically before continuing. "He has said you are the chosen one. You, my dear, will have the privilege of shaking his hand."

The other attendees murmured their approval at this news. Taken aback, Orla could only stutter. "What do I need to do?"

"You'll be guided by Melvin when the time comes."

Carron turned and addressed the rest of the company. "I have also been made aware that the rare phenomena of spiritual apports from inside my body will be witnessed this evening."

The other sitters enthusiastically received this announcement, which was accompanied by a variety of 'Oohs' and 'Ahhs'.

"But now I must go and prepare myself for what promises to be a wonderful night."

She left, and I felt like I'd just watched an actor exiting the stage.

Gertie and I returned to the apartment and were soon joined by Orla and Enya. Matty trailed in last, and Dorcas was still out by the pool.

"So are we going to this séance tonight?" Someone asked.

We decided we would attend. Everyone else except us seemed happy with last night, including Steve, the nice man from Yorkshire who assured us he'd had a fantastic night and was looking forward to this evening's event. Perhaps the problem lay with us, and anyway, Orla had been picked to take part. Dorcas, who had returned to the apartment by now, had no reservations and quipped that our negative energy might affect our perceptions. To which Gertie quickly retorted, "Yeah, right. Having negative energy makes you misunderstand what is being said in a language yet unknown to man."

Turning stiffly, Dorcas went back out to the pool.

That evening, we assembled at the séance room and, after removing anything metal, sat where we had sat the night before. Once settled, Carron came in dressed in flowing black robes and a matching turban. The heady scent of Honeysuckle followed and hung in the air as she went and sat in the chair. Steve witnessed Carron being strapped in, and I braced myself for the loud music.

Melvin informed us that Carron would be sitting in the cabinet building the power as the music played, that ectoplasm would come from her mouth and that under no circumstances was anyone to touch it because it could kill her "just like that". He snapped his fingers to emphasise the point.

The music was predictably loud, and went on to the point where it became uncomfortable. It stopped suddenly, a red light went on, and Melvin's voice told us he would now open the curtains on the cabinet so we could view the ectoplasm.

The curtains were pulled back, and Carron's head was to one side. She appeared to be asleep, and from her mouth and trailing down over her chest was what we had been told was ectoplasm. It looked for all the world like cheesecloth to me, but I reasoned that it could be what ectoplasm looked like, as I'd never seen it before. Gertie would later say it reminded her of a tea towel she had at home.

After we'd all seen this, the curtains were closed again, and what looked like dry ice appeared from under the curtains. Melvin assured us this was the start of the hand manifesting and cautioned Orla to be ready to come up and shake the hand of the Spirit.

Watching closely with only a low red light for illumination, it wasn't easy to see anything in great detail. The dry ice continued, and a white, glowing human hand appeared from its midst at floor level. There were gasps and comments from the sitters, and Melvin directed Orla to make her way to the cabinet. She squatted down, and we saw her take the hand in hers and initially pull back, then hold it again. A couple of minutes later, she was returned to her seat.

The hand retracted, and the 'dry ice' disappeared. A noise came from the cabinet, and someone pulled back the curtain. Carron called for a drink, and an open bottle of beer was given to her. She appeared to drink deeply, tipping the bottle right up, but the bit of light available shone through the green glass and revealed things floating in the beer.

Suddenly, Carron appeared to be choking, and a few sitters expressed concern. Then, from her mouth, she began to spit small coloured gemstones. Melvin informed us these were of spiritual origins and produced by ectoplasm inside Carron's body. They were gifts for us from the Spirit.

Surely, I wasn't the only one to have seen the 'spiritual gems' in the beer? It was evident to me that Carron had taken them into her mouth when she appeared to drink from the bottle. By now, I was feeling a little annoyed; the room got darker as the red light went off, and a soft drumming noise was heard somewhere in the room. The sound grew, and someone cried, "The Indians are coming."

The air above us became disturbed as if something was moving through it at speed. Enya yelled that she had been hit in the eye. Melvin responded, "Probably a mosquito," followed by Gertie's quick retort, "Don't you mean a tea towel?" I don't think Melvin heard that bit.

We didn't hang around when the event ended, but returned to the apartment. Something had undoubtedly hit Enya's eye, which was now red and watering. Orla was questioned at length about the hand that she had held.

She said, "It was a man's hand, and the pinky finger was missing the end."

"What did it feel like?" Matty asked.

"It was hairy," Orla replied, "and felt wet, like it was sweating."

"Perhaps that was the ectoplasm," Dorcas interjected. "Did

it smell?"

"I didn't get my face that close," Orla said, "but what I don't understand is that we weren't allowed to touch the ectoplasm coming out of Carron's mouth, but it was okay to touch the hand that was being produced from the same thing."

"Perhaps that's because the hand wasn't ectoplasm at all," Gertie said.

We all looked at her.

"To be honest," she continued, "I smell Bullshit. I think this whole weekend has been a sham; nothing we have seen has anything remotely to do with the Spirit world. What the heck was she doing, spitting them stones up? How in any way is that evidence for survival?"

Then, I revealed that I'd seen what looked like small stones in the beer bottle.

"There you have it," Gertie said triumphantly. "It was a green bottle, so you couldn't see inside where the so called gems were. Thats why she appeared to drain the bottle. The gems were at the bottom and she was tipping them into her mouth. Not very subtle is it? If you are going to cheat once surely everything is then called into question. I think we've been had."

We all sat looking at each other, knowing that Gertie was right, and we all felt a bit stupid. That is except for Dorcas, who maintained that what we had seen was actual spiritual activity and that we couldn't handle the truth when we saw it before going off to bed in a huff. Soon after, there was a knock at the door, and Don was there. He came in and appeared very upbeat. He smiled and said, "Well, what did you think of that? Pretty amazing stuff, eh?"

Awkward.

"Great. Just great," I remarked sarcastically. "We've certainly seen some things this weekend that have made us think. It's been a real eye-opener for all of us. I'm disappointed, though, that factual evidence seemed thin on the ground."

The sarcasm was lost on Don, and he chose to ignore the comment about factual evidence but seemed apparently otherwise happy with my reply. He left soon after confirming our departure time the following morning. He had offered us another night's stay and séance. Still, we declined politely, using Enya's morning sickness as an excuse to leave early. Whilst he was there, Orla was rolling her eyes and seemed agitated and, as soon as he had left, blurted out, "Did you see that?"

"What?" we all said in unison.

"His hands are hairy, and it looks like he's missing the top of his pinkie!"

"So his was the manifested hand," said Gertie, going into Miss Marple mode. "With the curtains shut, we couldn't see that he was in the curtained-off bit with Carron, and I bet the overly loud music is to cover the sound of him shuffling about."

We talked for a long time. Confused by the other sitters who seemed to have no reservations about the séances, we wondered if they were a part of the sham or merely deluded. Eventually, after talking long into the night, we accepted that we could trust nothing that had happened that weekend.

By 10 o'clock the next day, we were driving away from Sanctuaire de Raphael and heading home. As Don and Melvin waved us off, I saw that Orla was correct; the end of Don's pinkie finger was indeed missing.

Trance Night Revelations

Back home, lighter in pocket and disappointed, there was much to consider. Had all those books lovingly collected and read over the years been based on self-deception and lies? Were all those sitters who had written glowingly about séances deluded?

When I told him about our adventure, Obie's snort of derision was predictable; it supported his theory that everything related to mediums was fraudulent. He laughed at the absurdity of it and berated us for not doing some fact-finding before we went. Howard, now back from Japan, was politer, but an ill-hidden smirk betrayed his amusement as I indignantly ranted that, "It was like attending a pantomime!"

"You can't reject all those other accounts just because of one that appears to be fraudulent. What, if anything, did it teach you?"

"Not to be so bloody gullible," I said wryly. "We're all feeling a bit foolish; Cassie would find it really funny that we got ripped off because, ultimately, we were partially responsible. Obie is right. We were negligent in checking it out; we dove right in and got burned. Since returning, we've done a bit of exploring on the net, which, had we done before booking, we wouldn't have gone near France; the word fraud has cropped up a lot in connection with Carron and Melvin from a number of sources. Sadly, this mediumship does attract charlatans."

"It's not mediumship, though, is it?" Howard replied. "Be careful not to mix the two lest you tarnish one. You just got taken. It's bad luck, but surely it isn't the end of the world? Don't beat yourself up. It sounds to me like they've done it before. Your saving grace was that you all quite quickly realised something wasn't right."

"Except Dorcas," I interjected. "She still believes everything in the séance room was genuine."

"You can't make people see what they don't want to see. So dust yourselves down, dry your eyes, and put it down to experience."

Howard was right, and as time passed, we eventually felt less wounded and were able to laugh at our naivety. But for a while, it made us wary of exploring physical mediumship. Only we couldn't escape the reality that during our home circle, we had begun experiencing inexplicable noises, taps, lights and, on occasion, voices. A series of random photographs taken one night piqued our interest. They showed what appeared to be smoke coming from Orla's mouth as she meditated. We wondered if we were being led towards exploring physical mediumship.

Orla and I were drinking coffee one afternoon when our conversation turned to the direction the circle was going. We both agreed it was exciting and resolved to stay focused and to discern what we accepted as evidence. If a phenomenon was going to happen, we needed to know it was genuine. We would search for mundane reasons first for anything we might experience.

The recent visit to France made us realise how easily people could be deluded. Could we trust ourselves to be objective and not accept everything as coming from the spirit world? Irrefutable proof that could be corroborated was needed. It had to stand on its own merit, be unknown to anyone in the circle, be witnessed by us all, and be validated elsewhere.

As we agreed, that was the way to go; a penny dropped between us, apparently from out of nowhere!

Writing that sounds crazy. We looked up. Above us was nothing more than a bare white ceiling. Yet we had both seen the coin drop between us. Orla and I looked at each other, our eyes wide. We leaned forward to see where it had landed. She picked it up from the floor. It was unremarkable, just an ordinary penny, but one that had seemingly fallen from the air. Attempts to find where it had come from yielded no satisfactory explanation.

There are many accounts of similar incidents, and stuff indeed went missing and reappeared when Cassie first died. Still, there was always the question of whether I was being absent-minded. I'd never actually seen them occur, yet one just had in my brightly lit sitting room.

"It's a sign," Orla said. "The penny has dropped! Literally. Think what we were discussing. It's an affirmation. We need to test the spirits!"

The next time our circle sat, we collectively set the intention that we would be given information that we had no prior knowledge of and that it would be checkable to prove to ourselves that we should continue exploring this form of mediumship.

Some months later, on Sunday, 13th November 2022, Gertie travelled from her home in Birmingham to sit for our physical night. During the day, she and I lunched at a medieval hotel locally associated with the ghost of Mary Queen of Scots. Upon leaving, we found the main road out of the small market town was blocked in anticipation of a Remembrance Day parade.

Being familiar with the area, I knew eventually that I'd find a road that would lead us home, but it would mean taking a detour; we set off through stunning countryside resplendent in autumnal gold and reds.

Chattering and admiring the scenery, we eventually found ourselves in an idyllic chocolate box village. There was a pub on a green with a duck pond, thatched cottages adorned with window boxes lined narrow streets, and peacocks walked without care through well-kept gardens. Recognition dawned as we drove slowly through the tiny village, and I blurted out, "Oh, I know where we are; this is the Murder Cottage village."

Gertie looked at me, amused. "Murder Cottage? What's that all about?"

"Oh, I came here once with Obie about twenty years ago. I don't know what this place is called, but it has stuck in my memory because it is so beautiful, like stepping back in time. There's a particular cottage that I want you to see. I fell in love with it; it's utterly delightful. When he and I drove through, Obie called it the Murder Cottage. He said he'd always known it as that but didn't know why it had such a dreadful title."

We drove to the edge of the small hamlet where the cottage, West Lodge, sat perfectly in a clearing. Time hadn't dimmed my recollection; it was as lovely as I remembered. Its roof was blanketed in thick thatch that hung low, fringing the mullioned windows. Large trees gave shade to the garden, where a peacock elegantly occupied an empty swing amidst a fiery sea of red and bronze Rudbeckia blooms. Deep borders of pink Cosmos flowers swayed with a soft, ethereal beauty in the autumn breeze, inviting the eye to follow the gated path to the cottage's rustic red door. We parked and took some time to drink in the loveliness of this quintessential English country cottage.

"I see what you mean," said Gertie as we sat smoking.

"Yeah." I replied wistfully, "Right now I have dwelling envy."

We laughed, finished our cigarettes, and, without really knowing where we were going, drove out of the village and took a left. A few miles further along, we arrived in Fotheringhay. Infamous as the place Mary Queen of Scots was murdered by her cousin, Queen Elizabeth I. The church was open, so we explored its historically fascinating associations with Richard III and the House of York before heading home.

That evening, under a red light, our circle sat for one hour. As was usual, afterwards, we discussed anything that had happened during that hour. Gertie had brought forth the names Ashton and George whilst in a trance.

Believing those names might be important, Enya searched Google, but there wasn't much to go on. Although she didn't find anyone of that name, the search engine threw up a result that showed a record of George Peach, who, in 1952, with his wife Lillian, was beaten to death at their home in the sleepy hamlet of Ashton. Their assailant was never caught.

When Enya read out the details, I realised that Ashton was the village Gertie and I had driven through that afternoon.

"That's where the murder cottage is!" I exclaimed before telling the others about it.

"What if George was murdered in West Lodge, and that's why Obie used that horrible name?"

Enya, by now, had found a website about unsolved murders, which provided a picture of where the couple was slain. My blood ran cold. It was the same cottage. Further details showed that George had lived most of his life in Fotheringhay, only moving to Ashton six years before his death. He married Lillian in the church we had explored, and both were buried in the graveyard we had stood beside earlier in the day.

Was it all a coincidence that the road had been blocked and I had to make a detour? What had taken us to Ashton, Fotheringhay, and to the church that would have been so familiar to George?

I had no prior intention of visiting either, yet I found myself in both. Gertie was unfamiliar with the area we had visited. The chances of her mind being tainted with prior knowledge of a little-known and, by now, long-forgotten murder case were remote. Neither she nor I could have snatched the name from the grave of George and Lillian whilst visiting the church because we never entered the graveyard. We were more concerned with the interior architecture and history of the building.

I spoke to Obie, who confirmed that he was unaware of the details we had discovered. As much as we tried to debunk the course of events as a mere coincidence, we failed. Two names uttered from an entranced medium had revealed a dreadful course of events that, until that night, was unknown to anyone in the circle.

Perhaps most interestingly, on 13th November 1952, the police had a minor breakthrough when Lillian's bloodstained purse was found discarded in the village. We checked the date, and it was 70 years to the day we were sitting in the circle.

We all agreed the challenge we'd set had been cleverly met.

A Spirit Calls

A few days later, I was excitedly discussing 'The Murder Cottage incident,' as it became known, with Howard on what had become regular Zoom meet-ups. He was intrigued by how it had all come together and happy that it had satisfactorily fulfilled our requests.

"Did it prove anything?" He asked

"Yeah it shows that those in spirit are more involved in our lives than we are conscious of. And that I've been so wrong about something." I said. "I was told never to ask the spirit world for help."

"Why ever not?"

"Because we have to live our lives and learn our own lessons, and that they aren't allowed to interfere. I was told that nugget by someone who was as ill-informed as I appear to be."

"That sounds like rubbish." Howard snorted, "When you visit a medium looking for a message, aren't you looking for help?"

"I hadn't thought of it like that but yes. Indeed, among the stories I have, the suggestion is that rather than being unable or unwilling to 'interfere,' they can and do intervene directly without any plea for help."

"How so?"

"In various ways, vivid dreams for example and manipulation of technology, phones in particular."

"Interesting, I'd love to hear them but can they be verified by third parties?"

"They absolutely can," I replied with more than a smidgen of satisfaction.

"In fact, three days ago, one arrived from someone I knew from school who recently reached out to me via social media. We chatted briefly, filling in the gaps in our lives. She's now retired from the Health Service. When I told her I collected stories about spirit contact, she immediately said, "I've got a story." And she has, and it's remarkable. She emailed me it."

"Hold everything," Howard requested. "I need fresh coffee for this."

"Okay, I'll find the email she sent."

Howard was soon back, steaming cup in hand.

"Okay fire away." he said

"I'll read it as she sent it." I replied, continuing,

"Hi, Hannah,

"It's great to hook up with you again after all these years. Haven't we gotten old?

"When you said you were collecting stories, it reminded me of something that happened many years ago, which I still can't explain.

"I was 23, not long after I moved to Liverpool and started training as an ambulance driver. I was partnered with an experienced guy named Dave, whom I married two years after this event. He's sitting here now, and I can feel his gaze fixed on me as I type these words. Our memory of that night is as vivid as ever.

"It was around 3 a.m., a tranquil night, and we were having a break in the ambulance when the dispatcher alerted us that she had received a call from a personal alarm company.

"An alarm had gone off and when the company rang the telephone a woman answered, gave her name and said that her husband had fallen and needed help getting up. No other family contacts were on file, and the dispatcher asked if we would pop around and assess the situation; the police were also on their way. The file held details of where a key could be accessed if needed.

"When we pulled up outside, the Victorian terrace house was in darkness. The police arrived seconds after us. We knocked on the door, but there was no reply or sound of movement from inside. The copper radioed the dispatcher for the whereabouts of the key, and with that and torches, we made our way in.

"As we entered, we turned on the hallway light, revealing a time capsule packed with antiques and vintage furniture. Scattered around were cardboard boxes half full of knick-knacks.

"The policeman shouted, "Hello, is anyone here?"

"We heard a frail voice coming from upstairs and followed its direction. In one bedroom, where more boxes were scattered, we found an elderly gent with a plaster cast on his arm wedged between the bed and the wall, unable to move. After a quick assessment, Dave and I lifted him off the floor and sat him on his bed.

"He said he was going to the bathroom when he tripped over something, lost his balance, and fell. He began apologising to us for the boxes lying around. He mentioned his wife of many years, who had recently died, and he still couldn't bring himself to clear away her things. Thanking us profusely, he asked. "How did you know to come to my house?"

"I told him we had received a personal alarm alert from his home. He looked at me and spoke. "That's strange. My alert button is downstairs. I need to remember to bring it up. Muriel (his wife), always told me to keep it on me."

"Dave stayed upstairs and took the old fella to the toilet while the attending police officer and I went downstairs. I found the alert button on a hallway table next to the house phone (there were no mobiles back then). I called the alarm company and confirmed that the resident was fine now and had received help.

"I asked who she had spoken to, and she said she called the residence to ensure it wasn't an accidental trip; a woman named Muriel answered the phone and told her that her husband had fallen and needed help getting up, so she alerted us.

"And yet the man had told me only moments before that his Muriel had been dead for at least three months, and he was in the house alone.

"Now, Hannah, you've got to admit that is weird."

I looked up from reading; Howard was smiling.

"Yep, that is weird, and compelling," he said. "It blows your theory about non-intervention right out of the water."

We chatted some more about the inventive ways appliances and technology, the telephone in particular, seemed to be a popular choice of the spirit world to let us know they are still around with calls from defunct phones or numbers that don't exist. I went on to tell him about Bernhard, who had contacted me with the following:

"My mother died in 1991, and afterwards, I continued to live on our farm with my father. I was still living there in 2018, and one day my father and I were sitting in the kitchen; he was doing a crossword puzzle, and I was reading a book. His new mobile phone, which I had purchased for him the day before, was on the table. Only I had his telephone number, so we were surprised when the phone rang. He answered, and I saw a look of shock on his face. He passed the phone to me. I could hear a lot of static and my mother's voice asking, "Andre (my father), can you hear me?" The voice seemed to be coming from a great distance and was fading away.

"When the call ended, I redialed the number on the mobile screen, only to be informed that the number did not exist! The same thing happened again about a year later, around the anniversary of my mother's passing; I would not have believed it if I had not been there and heard her voice."

"They're clever aren't they?" Howard said.

We both agreed that such incidences suggested there was an intelligence at work that we weren't aware of, and concluded that it all felt very typical of what we here in the physical would do. Having landed safely on the other side, the one who has passed is keen to show those they love that they are okay, a bit like when we go on holiday and let the folks at home know we arrived safely.

"Oh, by the way," I said, "I have some news. I'm going to publish the stories - with the owner's permission, of course."

Howard, who was comfortable teasing me by now, smiled broadly. "About time! I was scared I was going to have to die myself and put in an appearance like Marley's ghost with dire warnings about your soul. You've been so adamant that you wouldn't, so what changed your mind?"

"I realised early on that the stories were helping me cope with grief. Some people climb mountains or run marathons, which is far too energetic for me. Instead, I've been collecting beautiful stories, generously shared, that support my belief that we can't die. Each story has helped me; they can help others. I see that now."

Howard was thrilled. After offering his help, he said, "Any idea what it might be called?"

"Geez, Howard let me get started first!"

Everyone has a Story

As I began the job of sorting the stories, it seemed as if most people I spoke to had experienced something they found inexplicable but, given the opportunity, were happy to tell it to ears willing to listen without judgment. So when a young friend, Stuart, who had zero interest in anything supernatural, visited me and said "something peculiar happened last week. I wonder if you can help me make sense of it," it naturally grabbed my attention.

"Yeah what was that?"

"I woke in the night, but it wasn't like I was wide awake; I felt groggy and sat up. I glanced at my clock, which said 1.30, and clearly saw my mate Alan from work standing in the corner of my room, looking around confused as if he didn't know where he was.

"The weird part is that something – I don't know what – was vibrating in the room, like a buzzing noise. Alan looked at me, then just disappeared, and the buzzing stopped. I wasn't scared, but it was surreal, and I went straight back to sleep.

"The following day, I didn't think much about it other than I had had a strange dream. It soon became apparent that something was off when I got to work, and there wasn't the usual bloke banter to greet me. Then, one of the lads said Alan had died the night before when his motorbike was hit by a lorry as he was travelling up the A1. He was catapulted off, and found over a branch of a tree not far from my flat."

"My god, that's dreadful," I said, handing Stuart a cup of coffee.

"Yeah, it's gutting; he was a nice man, we got on really well. It's odd, because according to the timings, I saw him about ten minutes after the accident. My clock is always set fifteen minutes fast. I glanced at it when I woke, and it said 1.30, so it was actually 1.15. According to his wife the accident was called in to the emergency services at 1.05 by a driver who was behind the lorry, and saw it happen. Why would I dream about him on the night he dies? I don't normally dream about my workmates and why was he confused?"

"Wouldn't you be confused if you found yourself in your mate's room when you had just been riding up the road in the middle of the night?" I replied.

"I guess so, but why was he in my room?"

"I wish I could answer that," I said, "but I can't. Perhaps Alan was killed immediately, but wasn't aware he was dead. Maybe he was trying to make sense of the situation and looking for something or someone familiar and ended up in your room because you guys were friends and your flat is near the accident site. I don't think it was a dream."

I went on to tell him about a friend of mine, Michelle, who walked into a tent where a band was playing at a weekend music festival she attended and saw her boss on the stage playing the guitar. She was surprised because she knew he had said he was attending a family event in Portugal that weekend.

Startled to see her boss, Michelle drew her companion's

attention to the stage, and her friend saw him, too. The guitarist looked at them, but his face changed, and her boss's face had gone. Michelle remembers experiencing a 'weird feeling' when she saw him. The following Monday, she went to work only to be told her boss was dead. Lightning struck him in Portugal during a freak storm. Further enquiries showed the accident occurred close to the time Michelle entered the tent.

Looking thoughtful, Stuart said, "Wow, that shit is weird. I thought I had just imagined it."

"It looks like you experienced a crisis apparition. Such events do seem bizarre," I said, "yet they don't seem rare. The opposite, in fact. From what I've read, there are thousands of reports of people seeing or sensing friends or relatives around the time of their passing.

"Like you, those who witness these events are unaware that the person has passed away until later. Quite why or how they happen is beyond my understanding; perhaps it's down to telepathy that allows some people to observe such things. They are fascinating nonetheless."

My young friend seemed satisfied with my explanation, as inadequate as I felt it to be. Like Michelle, he had a professional and friendly relationship with the deceased. Was it something about their respective relationships that drew the spirits of their friends to them at their time of passing?

I understood why these events might happen to those with deep personal connections to the deceased but also learned they can be witnessed by people with little or no emotional association with the departed, as happened to Alex, a rational, logical-minded friend who has a healthy scepticism about an afterlife. After I had told him what I was researching, I received the following:

"As promised, this is the experience I told you about at Sue Ryder Hospice.

"I had been visiting the Hospice for a few weeks, following my close friend's admittance due to his terminal diagnosis. Over various visits, I got to know some other residents, their families and the excellent doctors and nurses in attendance. On this particular day, I went to see him. As it was a hot summer morning, we sat outside his room overlooking the gardens, enjoying the sunshine and chatting away.

"He soon became fatigued, so I suggested he take a nap and I would stay outside for a while. Whilst he was resting, I reviewed some job applications and checked my social media.

"I looked up and saw another patient, Jim, coming out of his room, which was next door to my friend's. I was surprised to see him as I was aware he was bed-bound and in the final stages of his cancer journey. My friend and I had got to know him and his family on their regular visits to see him.

"As he passed me, I shouted, "Morning, Jim." He turned around, waved in acknowledgement, and continued walking. I thought no more of it until I heard some noise coming from his room soon after.

"The door to Jim's room opened, and his brother appeared clutching his telephone, looking visibly upset. I looked up and asked him if everything was ok. He explained that Jim had just passed away 10 minutes earlier, and now he had to do the ring around to various family members.

"Despite the warm sunshine, I felt cold inside. What had just happened? I had clearly seen him 10 minutes previously. He had passed me and had acknowledged my hello. My rational mind sparked into overdrive. What had just happened there?

"It felt authentic to me. I knew I had seen Jim, albeit surprised to see him looking so well, knowing he had been so poorly and could not get out of bed. Physically, he looked the same. Still, with hindsight, he was standing tall and upright, which I had never seen him do. He did walk past me, but it didn't occur to me that he was on a pathway that led to a dead end.

"Unsure of what I had witnessed, the experience didn't scare me. I felt privileged to have been the last person Jim had seen on earth. While I remain an interested sceptic, that event has reassured me that there is more to life and death than we currently know."

Did Alex see the spirit of a man walking away from his body, which was now useless to him? It certainly sounds like it. Alex's story joined my growing collection, and it became evident that interactions happened regardless of time or place.

Coming Together

I assembled the stories whilst picking Howard's brain whenever possible. Doubt plagued me, but things happened often that made me think I should carry on, and that stories wanted to be heard. Many hard decisions had to be made. I couldn't include them all, and Howard's advice was invaluable.

Each story was as unique as the person who told it to me, but all shared similarities. I haven't read one that was anything less than loving and positive. The beneficiaries all received exactly what they needed at the time, even when they didn't realise they needed it.

Like the one from a member of the armed forces, who swears that when he became trapped underwater on a training exercise, he was pulled bodily from the submerged vehicle by 'two tall shining beings', which was "impossible due to space restrictions in the cockpit". Yet he maintains they stood either side of him and "yanked me out".

His fellow crewmen, unaware of his dilemma, witnessed the event and commented later that he shot out the water "like you had a rocket up your ass." Sadly, he felt he was unable to share with them what had really happened for fear of ridicule.

Another comes from our circle member, Gertie. Her mother had recently passed away, and Gertie was tasked with putting her affairs in order, including clearing her house and belongings. One day, while at the house, she and her husband heard loud music coming, apparently, from next door.

Gertie moaned about the noise and commented that she hoped her late mother hadn't had to endure that too much. As the pair continued to put things in boxes, they realised that the music was actually drifting down the hallway from somewhere upstairs.

Thinking someone was up there, she and her husband followed the sound and opened the door of a bedroom where the music seemed to be coming from. Inside, a CD player with no discernable power source was lit up, playing a favourite track of Gertie's.

She filmed and retained the footage and showed it to me. What is clearly apparent is the joy in her voice as she sings along with this lovely sign from her mother.

These are stories that should be celebrated, not remain unheard.

Vivid dreams of the deceased seem to be more common in the early months following a passing. Unlike ordinary dreams, they are lucid, meaningful, and memorable. They involve the deceased and focus on giving reassurance that they are well. I have collected many accounts of such dreams, and all the recipients reported feeling comfortable with them. Whilst they cannot be validated by other sources, they nevertheless deserve a mention because they are so commonplace.

Prophetic dreams are rarer and appear to be random.

However, they can be so impactful that they cause the recipient to act upon them. What is more, the results of these 'dreams' can be endorsed by others.

A friend, Ankit, from Jaipur, India, related the following to me. His mother had a dream that appears to have averted a family tragedy. In October 2004, she dreamt of her own (deceased) mother urging the family to run, and of then seeing the entire family shouting for help before being swept away in a torrent of water.

The dream made such an impression on his mother that, much to the family's disappointment, she cancelled a planned trip to the Andaman and Nicobar Islands during the upcoming Christmas holidays. She refused point blank to go, saying it was a warning sent by God. Her insistence meant three generations of the family went somewhat grudgingly to Shimla instead.

On December 26th of that year, an undersea earthquake occurred along Northern Sumatra and the Nicobar and Andaman Islands, resulting in what became known as the 'Boxing Day Tsunami'. Without the dream, Ankit's entire family would have been holidaying just north of the earthquake epicentre and would likely have been caught up in what became one of the deadliest natural disasters in recorded history.

Perhaps those in the spirit world can more readily impact our consciousness in our sleep state. Why more people weren't warned of the impending tragedy remains unanswered. It could be that others had similar dreams and chose to ignore them or regarded them as 'just dreams' and not worthy of note.

One lady's insistence that she wasn't 'just dreaming' was Angie, who received a timely warning from her deceased mother-in-law:

"In June 1975, my husband, my two children, and I moved to my husband's home country of Italy from the UK. Towards the end of July, I was awoken in the early morning hours by my deceased mother-in-law's voice pleading for me to wake up. When I opened my eyes, she was standing as clearly as day on my side at the foot of the bed. Shocked and unable to move, I nevertheless felt a sense of peace and love. She looked young, just as she did the day I first met her many years before.

"It was impossible, yes, but undeniably she was there. She said, "Don't be frightened. I'm here to warn you that there's another key. Move the money. You and my son worked hard for it. Do as I ask, and remember I'll always love you, my son, and the children." With that, she was gone.

"Once I could move again, I woke my husband up and told him what had happened. He didn't believe me and said it must have been a dream, but I knew it wasn't.

"The following morning, concerned by the visitation (and because our entire savings, a substantial amount from selling our UK home, was in a chest in a nearby room), I left my children with my husband and went into town to open a bank account, where I deposited the money.

"Later, during lunch at my sister-in-law Elena's house, my husband mocked the events I had reported. Elena, however, was not as quick as my husband to reject what I had seen and suggested that there might be truth to it. She felt there was nothing to lose by calling 'their bluff', and the three of us returned to my house.

"The intense heat in Italy at that time of year was stifling and necessitated everyone to have a siesta. The village was deserted as everyone slept, but that afternoon, we all stayed up. We didn't have long to wait. Around mid-afternoon, as we sat out in the kitchen when we would usually be upstairs asleep, we heard the front door being unlocked quietly. We assumed only Elena, my husband, and I had a key, yet this person entering our home appeared to also have one.

"We sprang into action and ran to the under-stair passage by the front door and hid under the stairs. From there, we watched my other sister-in-law, Natalia, come in and enter the room, where she began to rummage through our belongings. In particular, the chest which held our bed linen, towels, and, until this morning, our entire savings!

"Natalia would have known the money was in the house because my husband shared such things with his sisters. However, she would have had no knowledge that the money had been moved.

"I absolutely believe my mother-in-law visited me. Taking heed of her warning halted what could have become a family tragedy. That money eventually paid for our permanent return to the UK on the advice of medics who told us my sick son couldn't be helped in Italy. My mother-in-law safeguarded our immediate future and that of my son. Ultimately, her daughter, who we discovered had secretly made a copy of the house key, was prevented from making a mistake she would regret later."

Both Ankit's mum and Angie listened to the warnings they were given, and potentially awful situations were seemingly averted. The question remains as to why some people receive such interventions, and others do not. We may never be able to reach a satisfactory answer. It might be that it is not for us to know such things but to be thankful and wonder at them when they do happen.

Love Was There First

"So you started collecting your stories to support what you had seen. Have they done that?" Howard asked as we were drinking coffee and chatting about the progress I was making in putting the stories together.

"Oh yes, undoubtedly," I replied, "but much more than that. I've learned so much and been surprised by a lot of things—more than I could have imagined when I started out."

"Like what?"

"I gained a greater understanding of why people are sceptical of such events. It's difficult to conceive of something that you've never experienced. I questioned my own incidents, and I was there!

"Another thing I have learned is that many people have had supernatural experiences. It's not rare, as I once thought. Again, I gained a greater understanding of why people are reluctant to discuss such things. No one wants to be perceived as unstable."

"Next question," Howard laughed, staring at me hard. "Has it helped with your grief?"

Until that moment, I had not realised how my focus on other people's stories had consumed most of my thinking. There was a pause, and then Howard gently asked. "You're not telling me something; what is it?"

I looked at my friend, knowing that he might, above all others, understand and relate to how I was feeling.

"Grief is a strange thing for sure," I replied. "It's been nearly six years, and even now, without warning, it sometimes jumps out of nowhere and bites me in the ass. A certain colour or the turn of someone's head, and just for a second, my heart flips and catches me unawares. It's understandable, but it's the mournful feeling I feel afterward that I don't want anymore."

"The tear in the eye, lump in throat thing?"

I nodded. "That's the one, sneaky, isn't it? When did it stop for you?"

"Sneaky is right, mine stopped after the reading in Glasgow, which was nearly ten years after the accident if my memory serves me correctly. Hannah, we grieve because love was there first, and we need to know we'll see them again. When we really know for sure that we will, grief has no place in our lives anymore. Something changes. We think of them without sadness. That knowledge gifts us a life that isn't marred by periods of melancholy."

"You would think, wouldn't you?" I went on," that all the research I've done and the numerous stories I've collected would be enough, but I'd like to hear from Cassie one time again. Is that selfish?"

"Selfish how? Don't be daft, what is selfish about wanting to hear how your bestie is doing. Sounds like you need to go see a medium."

"I have, plenty of times. And many times, I have had lovely messages, but like you, I want the gold standard and have yet to get it. I don't understand why I need that."

"If you get it, you'll know why you needed it. Do you even know what it is?"

I thought for a moment.

"Oh yeah. Something of substance that will knock my socks off, an accurate date, something I've seen or said last Thursday, that type of thing. Of course it's lovely being told that someone from spirit is bringing love but it proves nothing. God I sound like a spoiled child always wanting more don't I?"

"You might be waiting a long time," Howard interjected. "If you are meant to hear from her, it will happen, perhaps when you least expect it."

Suddenly, a loud squawking interrupted us. Howard jumped up quickly and disappeared from the screen, returning with a small bundle of black fur attached to his arm.

"What's that?" I asked.

"This is Shadow, aka the dark fiend, my sister's kitten. He's here while she's on holiday."

He held the kitten up to the screen, and two amber eyes stared back at me.

"He's adorable," I simpered.

"Undoubtedly, but with the claws of a tiger, he is determined to get into Barney, although I wouldn't rate his chances. That bird has a beak that could open a corned beef tin."

We chatted some more as the kitten nibbled Howard's collar before moving on to his beard.

"Of all the stories you have, do you have a favourite?" Howard asked.

"Oh yes, Buster's Butt," I laughed.

"Buster's Butt?" Howard was smiling.

I told him about Buster and how he had responded to healing. We conceded that although it wasn't technically about direct spirit intervention that was provable, it was nevertheless "an excellent outcome for everybody, especially Buster."

"Indeed, it is the best news." I said, "Oh, by the way, I'm off to Stansted to the Arthur Findlay College in May."

"Oh nice. Are you going to be doing a course?" Asked Howard.

"No," I replied. "It's an open day with a demonstration in the evening with Gordon Smith. I saw it online and booked; our circle is going."

"I've never been, have you?" Howard asked.

"No, this will be my first time, I've promised myself for years I'd go but never have and I'm really looking forward to it."

"And I look forward to hearing all about it."

By now, the kitten was getting busy nibbling Howard's ear.

"I think that's a hint that the fiend wants feeding. I'll call you next week for an update on the progress of your upcoming book. Do you have any idea yet what it might be called?"

"I haven't a clue. I'm awaiting inspiration."

A Violet Feather

"What does Violet mean for you?"

The question came from my friend Freya, who was staying with me for a few days. Matt had called in to see her, and the three of us were having afternoon tea and discussing, amongst other things, the book project. We were brainstorming potential titles that could capture the essence of these stories. Freya, knowing my love for colours had suggested we draw inspiration from them.

"Well, apart from it being a favourite colour of mine and it's association with the crown chakra," I replied, "my mind goes straight to our garden when I was a child. My mother loved the flowers so much and had a lot of primroses and violets. I recall her horror when I raided her flower beds and presented her with a posy of them, complete with their roots."

All at once, I remembered it was also Cassie's middle name. A name she thought dreadfully old-fashioned, which she hated, and made me promise never to call her by it. We had always taken the Mickey out of each other, so I ignored her request and took it upon myself to use it whenever possible just to annoy her. She would get so frustrated with me when she opened another birthday card addressed to Violet. She eventually accepted I wasn't going to let up, but insisted

"Just don't ever call me Vi!"

And I never did.

Amused by the memory, I related it to Freya and Matt and had a laugh at Cassie's expense. We continued to mull over title suggestions, and frustratingly, something felt wrong about them all. After what seemed like too long and at a loss, Matt jokingly said, "C'mon spirit, if you lot up there have any ideas, we're open to signs".

Matt got up to use the bathroom. When he returned, he was holding a beautiful large white feather.

"Where did you get that?" I asked.

"I've just found it in the middle of the hallway floor."

"Really?" I said, "I've only just walked through there and saw no feather."

"Well, I don't know how you missed it," Matt said.

"Oh, perhaps that's your sign," Freya said.

"Well, it's bloody quick if it is," I replied.

Freya looked over at me and grinned. "What about a Violet Feather?"

It was a special moment. My stomach flipped as Freya said those words, and we knew immediately that it was a fitting title. The combination of 'Violet,' representing my friendship with Cassie, and 'Feather,' symbolizing a spiritual presence, perfectly encapsulated the essence of the book.

Finding Gold

The day was bright and warm as Gertie, Matt, Michael - a new circle member - and I made our way to Stansted. Matt insisted on driving again. The journey of just over an hour was uneventful. We arrived at our destination around midday, and after grabbing a coffee, we set off to explore the imposing red brick Jacobean-style mansion that is the Arthur Findlay College.

We wandered into an interior as impressive as the architectural grandeur of the outside. Aged floors creaked underfoot as we passed through oak-panelled corridors lined with portraits. Tall glass windows, sweeping staircases and elaborately decorated Adam fireplaces drew our admiration. The house was full of visitors like us exploring their surroundings. There was a real buzz about the place as people hurried here and there.

The mansion, built in 1876, sits on land with a long history of occupation stretching back to Roman times. It rests quietly in the landscape embraced on all sides by nature. After lunch, we escaped the noise of the house to the estate's extensive grounds and woodlands, where we spent a gentle afternoon sitting in the warm sun, chatting, taking photos, and speculating how many mediums had studied on that spot over the years.

The day allowed us all to relax before the evening demonstration being held in the Sanctuary. The atmosphere was lively with chatter as we took our seats in the packed room. After a speech by the president, Gordon Smith was introduced, and his demonstration quickly began. He brought magical energy into the room, and both Gertie and I saw sparks of light around him. The first message was rapidly delivered to a woman at the front of the room. Next, he said that he had a woman with him who had died in 2017 on May 25th/26th and that she was coming through as a friend, not family. I felt a sharp dig in my ribs from Gertie.

"It's Cassie," she hissed.

I waited, raising my hand when further information came I knew was unique to my friend. I had crossed paths with Gordon at events and online but knew he couldn't know any of the personal details he was now giving me. The level of accuracy was extraordinary, including family names, and as he came to the end of the message, smiling, he pointed his finger at me, began wagging it and said,

"Oh, by the way, she says, 'Just don't call me Vi!'"

My head snapped over to where Matt was sitting. He was mouthing, "Wow," at me. I just sat there gobsmacked, with my heart racing. I had just got my gold standard.

Afterwards, outside in the stunning gardens, watching the sun go down over the countryside, Gertie and I stood smoking leant against an ornate balustrade.

"That was some evidence," she said. "Is the date accurate?"

"Spot on." I smiled. "There are 365 days in the year, and he picks the correct one. She died around midnight on the 25th but it was recorded by the doctor as 26th because that's when he saw her. And the whole "Don't call me Vi" thing—only Freya, Matt, and I knew about that!"

"And Cassie," Gertie said. "She must have been listening."

"That's unsurprising, she was always earwigging."

We looked at each other and began laughing.

"I'll never need another reading Gertie. I've just had all the evidence I could ever want; if that isn't proof, I don't know what is."

Relishing that particular moment, we finished our cigarettes in silence before joining Matt and Michael, who were waiting patiently in the car park.

A few days later, I was drinking my first coffee of the day and thinking about our Stansted trip. I no longer dreaded Cassie's imminent anniversary and the low mood that usually accompanied it.

Rather than believing, I now *knew* that death is merely a doorway. Beyond that doorway, our consciousness in some form exists, and continues its journey unabated in an existence we cannot yet conceive of. Yet, we can get snapshots of it and the people there through the work of credible mediums. If everyone was as privileged as I to receive such proof, the world would be a far happier place.

The early morning summer sun was streaming through my window, and at 7.30, my phone lit up with an incoming call. It was Cassie's daughter telling me her dad had died during the night. I was reminded of the similar call he had made to me precisely six years before, but there was no sadness this time; he'd found life hard without Cassie, and I knew they were together again.

That weekend, during meditation at an online workshop, I found myself looking across a wildflower meadow. A large Oak tree, its vibrant green canopy caressing the blue sky, sat off in the distance. Beyond that, a panorama of gently rolling hills seemed to go on forever. Under the tree was Cassie. Beside her were her husband and son and their dog, Wazza. She waved, and my thought was, "See ya later, gal."

As I watched them move off, from just behind my left ear, the mysterious but by now trusted and familiar voice that I first heard at the riverbank six years before spoke again.

It simply said,

"The Joy Continues."

Afterthoughts

Of course, Howard was delighted by my news when I spoke to him the following week. He was grinning widely, sitting relaxing on his plush sofa, with Digger and Dave snoring beside him. Barney was perched on his shoulder. On hearing my voice, the bird fixed his intense yellow eyes on me. I could sense the animosity exuding from him.

Like an excited child, I reported every detail of the recent events, relishing the way in which they had played out. Howard laughed and said, "It shifts paradigms, doesn't it?"

I hadn't stopped smiling since returning from Stansted, and I could hear that in my voice as I said,

"It really does. Something has changed, it's hard to understand the impact it can have. That message eliminated any uncertainty about seeing Cassie. I feel lighter for that. It made me recognise the importance of acknowledging and supporting people's unique experiences. If they say they have witnessed something, they probably have.

"The bereaved don't need anyone to speculate or dissect their after-death incidents, just someone to listen without judgment. Grief is complicated enough without the fear of believing you are going mad."

"I completely agree," Howard said, smiling. And I'm so happy you got your gold standard, too."

"Yeah, I had no expectations before going to Stansted, and until I got it, I didn't know what it was I sought, but my goodness, I'm so happy."

"I can see that. You are buzzing and you look radiant. Now you've found what you were looking for, what next for you?"

"Next? I haven't had time to think really. Finish putting the stories together. Enjoy life, have an adventure, and adopt another doggie, maybe. Who knows what opportunities might present themselves, and I'm ready to embrace them."

"That sounds great," Howard said. "I'm planning a trip to India to see my extended family. I should be there for about a month. A lot has happened over the past few years, but the most important thing I've learned is to enjoy the moment. What do you feel you've learned from all this?"

I thought for a moment before answering. "I think the overwhelming thing is that as a society, we could be kinder to our bereaved. Shockingly, there is no legal right to paid time off for bereavement here in the UK. Unpaid time is often a matter of days if the employer agrees. That only applies when it's an immediate family member. People are expected to 'get over it' as quickly as possible and move on when what they need is time.

"You and I both know that a few days is ridiculously inadequate. Grief doesn't pack up and leave when the funeral is over; often, that is when it really kicks in. So the bereaved are compelled to 'soldier on' or take sick leave, paid holiday or unpaid leave at a time when that's the last thing they need to think about."

I ended my rant and tried not to look at Barney, who I knew would be looking back. He unsettled me.

"I couldn't agree more," Howard said. "I was fortunate to have an understanding boss who allowed me all the time I needed. There's no way a few days is ever enough."

"The other thing is," I interjected, "I think we need to find fresh ways to think and speak about dying, death, and grieving. It's an integral part of living as much as any other. Yet, we seem to ignore it until it's on us, and few people are comfortable talking about it."

"How do we change that?" Howard asked.

"By talking about it in an open and honest way instead of it being something to be feared and not mentioned. After all, it will happen to us all."

Howard nodded in agreement and excused himself to make a coffee. He put Barney onto his perch behind the sofa. Not wanting to sit staring at him, I rose and headed for the kitchen.

"Piss off!" Barney squawked at my back as I walked away.

I chuckled to myself as I clicked on the coffee machine; that bird really had an attitude.

Howard returned, fresh coffee in hand, apologising for the outburst.

"I don't think he likes me, Howard," I said, smiling as I sat down with my fresh cup.

"Hannah, he hates everyone except me, particularly females. He called my mum a cow the other day. Being Hindu, she took it as a compliment."

After Howard had squeezed himself onto the sofa between Digger and Dave, and got himself comfortable, he asked.

"Do you think you'll return to counselling?"

"I'm afraid not," I admitted quickly. "I wouldn't feel right going back. Most counselling has no place for discussing an afterlife or experiences like yours or mine. I would be a hypocrite if I sat with a client who wanted to have that conversation and professional protocols wouldn't allow it. I would feel as if I were cheating them."

"So what's the answer?"

"For those who need or want it, talking therapy that is open to conversations about an afterlife alongside mediumship and healing is the way forward. Recently, I've seen the results of the three modalities in combination, and they were outstanding. A few people are offering this service, but sadly, there are too few."

"That sounds like an interesting idea." Howard smiled. "I recall needing a space to talk about Ruth and the boys, just to say their names and share our experiences. I was afraid to do so because I sensed people were uncomfortable hearing it. Most of all, I wanted somebody to listen to what I had experienced after the crash, just someone to say, "I believe you.""

"Didn't you even tell your mum about that?" I asked.

"No, like I've said before, I had never really mentioned it to anyone. I had touched on it with the counsellor, who shut it down immediately. There was no one at work I could talk to. Scientists deal with facts, and I was struggling to accept what I had experienced as fact. I was afraid they would think I had lost the plot.

"I kept the experience to myself and was happy with the outcome after the reading in Glasgow. If we hadn't met, it would have stayed that way. It's been interesting, especially discovering that my experience wasn't unique. I'm glad I chose that seat on the train."

"Same here. Which reminds me," I remarked, "why did you elect to sit there? The carriage was all but empty. You could have sat anywhere."

Howard looked back at me sheepishly and smiled.

"I wondered if you'd ever ask me that. It was a case of mistaken identity."

"How so?"

"I was sitting further down the train, and boy, it was noisy and full. I knew the first-class option was available and quieter, so that's how I ended up in that carriage. When I saw you, there was something familiar, and at first sight believed you were someone I knew who lived nearby. Of course, I quickly realised my mistake as I asked you if the seat was free."

"You do know I really didn't want you to sit there, don't you?"

"Well, I do now," he joked before continuing, "but it was the book on the table that stopped me from walking away. I recognised the medium on the cover, and something made me want to talk to you, so blame the book for my interruption!"

"How weird is that?" I responded. "I grabbed that book from the shelf without really thinking as I left that morning. I took it for the sole reason of hiding behind it determined I wasn't going to talk to anyone. And then you turned up."

"Weird? Do you really think so, Hannah? Or is it like you are so fond of saying, Spirit really does work in mysterious ways!?"

Acknowledgements

My heartfelt thanks go to all those people who submitted their experiences, and trusted me to include them here.

Thank you also to my friends, who helped me in so many different ways, for your unwavering love, support, and laughter that has been the fuel to my creative process.

You are all stars!

Hannah

Printed in France by Amazon
Brétigny-sur-Orge, FR